VOTER'S DILEMMA
Indian Political Scene

Dr. Janak Raj Jai
M.A., LL.M., Ph.D. (Law)
Advocate
Supreme Court of India

Regency Publications
New Delhi

Voter's Dilemma: Indian Political Scene

"For effective Governance, we must have quality leaders. And quality leadership can be provided by persons who are trained to look at things objectively.

Unless we have good leaders to represent the citizens of this country in the legislature or in the executive, we cannot have good governance."

Justice G.T. Nanavati
Judge
Supreme Court of India

ISBN 81-86030-65-4

Published by Regency Publications, 20/36-G, Old Market, West Patel Nagar, New Delhi 110 008 and printed at Radiant Printers, New Delhi, Phones: 574 0038, 571 2539; Telefax: 578 3571.

Dedicated
to the

VOTERS

of

FREE INDIA

PREFACE

The elections for the 12th Lok Sabha are going to commence from 16th February, 1998. The 11th Lok Sabha could not complete its full term and had to be dissolved prematurely. Within less than two years period, we have seen three governments at the Centre. On account of marriage of convenience, and alliance of opportunism, no government could function continuously even for a year. This type of situation, where rampant corruption, lawlessness and political and economic instability have become the order of the day, has completely shaken the confidence of the people of the country. The leaders of the country have miserably failed to give a stable and able governance, because they kept their personal interest above the interest of the country. In Justice M.C . Chagla's words, "the elected members do not represent the people, they represent the money power." And there is no doubt in my mind, that the people of our country will lose faith in cherished democratic values, if leaders of all political parties do not take prompt corrective measures to remedy this situation.

After the premature dissolution of the Parliament, the country's voter has again been pushed into the process of election for the 12th Lok Sabha. Taking into consideration the voter's dilemma, an earnest effort has been made in this book to address all possible questions, and to find out a permanent remedy to bring political and economic stability as also to strengthen the democracy, which has unfortunately been derailed by those who are supposed to be its custodians.

I show my gratitude to all those whose views have been highlighted in this book for the benefit of the voters. Avtar Singh Sohal's article, is very informative and thought provoking. The top industrialists also have shown keen interest in the stable,

able, smooth and peaceful running of the Government. Their valuable suggestions and outbursts are reproduced in the book.

Justice G.T. Nanavati's (sitting Judge of the Supreme Court) message for good governance also forms part of the present work. Justice P.B. Sawant, Chairman, Press Council of India and Dorali R. Sopariwala, Vice-chairman, MARG, have also expressed their views, which have been (approvingly) reproduced for the information of the voters.

The entire credit for writing of this book goes to the publisher, at whose instance and initiative I ventured to undertake this project. It was indeed a neck breaking exercise to complete this work in such a short span of time.

In the end, I show my indebtedness to S/Shri K.S. Bhati (Registrar, ILI), Arvind Kumar, K.C. Bajaj, Shashi Bhushan Jain, I.C. Kumar, Pramod Singh, Vishwanath, and all members of the Library Staff of the Indian Law Institute for every possible help they extended to me in the accomplishment of this book.

New Delhi — Dr. Janak Raj Jai
January, 1998
Sewa Sadan
C-50, Rajpur Khurd Colony,
New Delhi 110 068
Ph. 6803447, 6932057

*While I was writing the preface for the book, there was suddenly a flash on the TV, "**Justice M.M. Punchhi, has been appointed as the next Chief Justice of India**". I am mentioning this happy news here, as in Chapter 4 of the book, there is a reference about the controversy on the appointment of the next Chief Justice after Chief Justice J.S. Verma retires on 18th January, 1998.*

Author

CONTENTS

1

RIGHT TO VOTE

For an election, there must be persons who desire to be elected or who offer themselves for election. They are called candidates. There may be prescribed qualifications for being elected or disqualifications preventing them from contesting and being elected.

Office of Profit

One of the specific disqualifications for the membership of Parliament and State Legislature is the holding an 'Office of Profit' under the Government of India or the Government of any State. The underlying object of imposing disqualification on the ground of holding office of profit is that a person who is contesting election for membership of a legislature or who is a member of legislature, should not be indebted to Government for an office which carries profit and thus compromises his independence.

The right to contest elections to the Houses of Parliament and State Legislatures has been conferred on all citizens of India irrespective of caste, religion, creed, educational qualifications, ownership of property etc. This right is a statutory right and not a fundamental right, unlike the right to be registered as an elector, which is guaranteed by Constitution.

The right to vote or stand as a candidate is not a civil right, but is a creation of statute or special law and must be subject to the limitations imposed by it. (AIR 1952 S.C. 64—N.P. Ponnuswami vs. Returning Officer, Namakkal).

A candidate at an election has to satisfy the following qualifications:

i) A candidate should be a citizen of India.

ii) A candidate should not be less than thirty years of age in the case of election to Rajya Sabha and Legislative Council of a State and not less than twenty-five years in the case of election to Lok Sabha and the Legislative Assembly of State.

iii) A candidate has to take an oath or make a solemn affirmation to the effect that he shall bear true faith and allegiance to the Constitution of India and that he would uphold the sovereignty and integrity of India (Art. 84(a) and 173(a) of the Constitution).

Right to Vote

The right to vote has been conferred upon every person of both sexes, who is a citizen of India, and who is not less than 18 years of age.

Article 326 of the Constitution reads as under:

> The election to the House of People and to the Legislative Assembly of every state shall be on the basis of adult suffrage; that is to say, every person who is a citizen of India and who is not less than eighteen years of age on such date as may be fixed in that behalf by or under any law made by the appropriate legislature and is not otherwise disqualified under this Constitution or any law made by the appropriate legislature on the ground of non-residence, unsoundness of mind, crime or corrupt or illegal practice, shall be entitled to be registered as a voter at any such election.
>
> No person is to be registered in the electoral roll for more than one constituency, nor for one constituency more than once. No registered voter can vote at a general election in more than one constituency of the same class and if he does, his votes in all such constituencies shall be void.

Voting Age

Prior to the amendment as to the age of voting from 21 to 18, a seminar was organised to have a full-fledged debate on the subject. Among the supporters of reduction of voting age was Shri S.L. Shakdhar, the then Chief Election Commissioner. The Joint Parliamentary Committee on Amendments to Electoral Law had also recommended lowering of voting age, after considering the views of those of its members who did not favour a change. The all India political parties, with the exception of the Congress Party had also favoured lower age, and some of them had done so in their election manifestoes.

Among those who had not favoured lowering of voting age were the late M.C. Chagla, who thought that we needed mature voters, the late Rajni Patel, who felt that it was not yet time for lowering the age, C. Subramaniam who wanted a considered decision to be taken after watching the effect of the lowering of the age in UK and USA, and N.A. Palkhiwala who did not consider lowering of the voting age to be urgent. This was of course the minority view and thus could not prevail. The Joint Committee on Amendments to Election Law gives the reasons offered by them.

"The size of the electorate would increase to a tremendous extent partly as a consequence of inclusion of the persons in the age group 18–21 years and partly because of the considerable rate of increase of population. This would also introduce party politics in the educational institutions which would be a source of disturbance at regular intervals and would also distract the students from their studies. Above all it would create heavy financial burden on the exchequer for handling such a vast electorate."

But the majority view was in favour of reducing the age of voter from 21 to 18. The members rightly observed that the younger generation, who is the future of the country, would have a sense of participation in the democratic process. It was also felt that if a person at the age of 18 is considered major and is competent to handle all the affairs, including getting employment, entering into legally valid contracts etc., why can't he be considered fit to cast his vote, which is his constitutional, yet a most precious and valuable right. By reducing the voting age, we have at the same time, to be very careful in making this voting right practically effective. This right can only be helpful in the democratic process of the country, if the youth is properly enlightened with regard to the proper use of their vote for choosing only the right representative.

JP's Total Revolution through Youth and Students

It will be quite appropriate to mention here that Lok Nayak Jayaprakash Narain was able to bring total revolution in the country in 1975, only through the active participation of the youth and students. Let me refresh the memories of my countrymen by reminding them that Indira Gandhi imposed internal emergency in the year 1975 to perpetuate her authoritarian rule and lakhs of innocent persons including prominent leaders from her own party even like Morarji Desai, Chandra Shekhar, Bhim Sen Sachhar, Mohan Dharia, Krishan Kant etc. were sent to jail without knowing the hows and whys of their arrest. It was at that point of time that JP gave a call for a total revolution and the whole movement was made successful only with the main participation of the youth and students. And ultimately Janata Party Government came into existence overthrowing the government headed by Indira Gandhi.[1]

On lowering of age of voting, Subhash Kashyap, former Secretary General, Lok Sabha in one of his papers had said:

> 'Whereas in many important countries, the voting age had been brought down to 18 years, our Constitution did not give the right of vote to all adults but only to those who are 21 years of age or older, and thus the youth in the age group of 18–21 years are deprived of their share in the country's affairs; those in this group felt alienated and ignored, becoming 'outsiders' in the current politico-socio economic culture of the country. As 18 is recognised as the age of adulthood in law, it is an anarchronism that first class graduates are debarred from voting unless they get to be 21, while at the same elections 80–90 years old 'embodiments of reaction, senility and ignorance' (these are very harsh words, used, apparently to emphasise a point) are allowed to vote. That the system places such a high premium on age that an illiterate man above 21 has more rights than a university graduate of a lower age, that illiteracy being far more wide spread in the higher age groups than among those below 21 years, we are excluding from the field of politics a sizeable section of the educated population of the country, that during the 18–21 year period of life a person is full of high ideals; and that the demands of the societal force and the dictates of political sagacity make it essential that the 50 million young men and women should be given the right to vote without further delay'.

From various studies carried out in this respect, the majority view has been in favour of reducing the voting age from 21 to 18. Besides this, the countries where the voting age is 18 years include USA, UK, Canada, Australia, Newzealand, France, USSR and The People's Republic of China. On the Indian sub-continent, the only exception was Nepal. India has since amended the law and has reduced the voting age from 21 to 18.

So from whatever angle we may view the reduction in the age of voting from 21 to 18, it has been welcomed by almost all the sections of the society. Rajiv Gandhi Government certainly took an admirable decision and allowed the youth of the country to participate practically in shaping the destiny of our country. It goes without saying that the youth of our country at the age of 18 are not less mature and sensible than the youth similarly placed in all other countries which have a formalised universal suffrage.

According to the latest figures available our 5 crore students studying in 200 universities and 7,000 colleges, approximately 70 per cent of them are voters. If properly organised, they can be a strong and veritable vote bank. Thousands of them may belong to the youth wing of various political parties. Apart from the students organisations with affiliations to different political parties, there are various independent groups as well. If we are able to bring unity among them, they may become a big force to reckon with. Any government in power can under no circumstances ignore the problems the youth community suffers from. Happily the minds of the youth and students eligible to cast their votes, are at the moment still volatile and incorruptible. This unused and ignored human resource can certainly play a revolutionary role in the creation of desirable political atmosphere among the innocent, illiterate and ignorant voters. This virgin area unfortunately has yet not been touched by any political party in the acceleration of the democratic process. The youth thus may not only prove useful in election, but also in bringing awareness among the general people against corrupt politicians, bureaucrats and the ministers holding high positions in various departments.

A Million Dollar Question

Vote is a trust with every citizen, and it has to be utilised in an appropriate manner, taking into consideration the best interest of the country. With the mushroom growth of the political parties and the role of mafia which has taken over the electoral system, a great responsibility lies on the Election Commission of India as also on the general voter to give their country a stable and able government. The task is a gigantic one, and it has to be accomplished with all our might. The voter is indeed in a great dilemma and eagerly looks forward for right directions to cast his vote without fear or favour to the right person of his choice wedded to democratic principles. The Supreme Court also in its recent pronouncements has taken a serious note of violation of the public trust by certain men in high political offices.

An earnest effort has been made to deal with this most serious problem in the foregoing chapters of the book.

REFERENCE

1. Emergency Excesses — Daylight Robbery of Human Rights and JP the Saviour, by Dr. Janak Raj Jai, Regency Publications.

2

THE ELECTION COMMISSION OF INDIA

(Its Structure and Powers)

The preamble to the Constitution sets out the aims and aspirations of the people of India. The provisions of the Constitution of India contain all these aspirations. The ultimate aim of the framers of the Constitution was to have a welfare state and an egalitarian society protecting the aims and aspirations of the people of India who made every sacrifice to see the light of freedom.

All government organs and institutions owe their origin to the Constitution and derive their powers from its provisions. The preamble of the Constitution provides that it is the people of India who have enacted and given to themselves the Constitution.

The preamble of the Constitution reads:

We, the people of India, having solemnly resolved to constitute India into a Sovereign, Socialist, Secular Democratic Republic and to secure to all citizens;

Justice, social, economic and political;
Liberty of thought, expression, belief, faith and worship;
Equality of status and of opportunity;
and to promote among them all
Fraternity assuring the dignity of individual
and the unity and integrity of the Nation;

In our Constituent Assembly this twenty-sixth day of November 1949, DO HEREBY ADOPT, ENACT AND GIVE TO OURSELVES THIS CONSTITUTION.

Independent Agencies

The Constitution has devised certain independent authorities to deal with particular matters. They are (1) Comptroller and Auditor General of India (2) Election Commission of India and (3) Union Public Service Commission.

Election Commission of India: To ensure fair and impartial election, an independent Election Commission will be appointed by the President. The Commission shall be responsible for the preparation of electoral rolls and for the conduct of Election to Parliament and to the legislatures of states, and for the election of the President and the Vice-President of India.

Article 324 of the Constitution prescribes that superintendence, direction and control of election shall be vested in the Election Commission of India.

(1) The superintendence, direction and control of the preparation of the electoral rolls for and the conduct of all elections to Parliament and to the Legislature of every state and of election to the offices of President and Vice-President held under the Constitution shall be vested in a Commission (referred to in this Constitution and the Election Commission).
(2) The Election Commission shall consist of the Chief Election Commissioner and such number of other Election Commissioner, if any as the President may from time to time fix and the appointment of the Chief Election Commissioner shall subject to any provisions of law made in that behalf by Parliament, be made by the President.
(3) When any Election Commissioner is so appointed the Chief Election Commissioner shall act as Chairman of the Election Commission.

Until elections to the 11th Lok Sabha were held, there was only one Chief Election Commissioner; of course all the Chief Election Commissioners had been men of great ability and proven integrity. In no democratic country is the size of electorate at all comparable to that in India and apart from that, ours is the only Election Commission which has jurisdiction over State as well as Union Election.

In USA, the Federal Election, is not at all concerned with the State Elections, most of the States have their own bipartisan Commissions. In France, the National Supervisory Commission, set up on the eve of an election campaign, has its responsibilities limited to ensuring fairness and proper observation of the relevant rules for the election of the President only, it does not concern itself with other elections. It consists of the Vice-President of the Consoll d' Estat (the highest administrative court) who acts as the Chairman of Commission, the first president of court of cessation and the first President of the Audit Court, and to active or honorary members of one or other three courts appointed by the three statutory members.

Our Election Commission has thus a far wider jurisdiction and responsibilities than the Election Commission in any other democratic country. Happily inspite of recommendation of the earlier Chief Election Commissioners, we have now a multi member Election Commission.

The Election Commission of India has to look after a variety of administrative matters and practical problems, as also to maintain contact with the administrative authorities at the Centre as well as in the States of the country. The Commission has also to perform quasi judicial function, over and above all this, the Commission has the responsibility of overseeing the entire electoral process. In three member Commission as is the present situation, the Chief Election Commissioner would be the Chairman as the Constitution also provides and would act as the effectual leader and coordinator, and has the overall responsibility for the working of the Commission. Whatever may be structure of the Commission and howsoever adequate may be the powers conferred on it, its effectiveness requiring use of influence as well as power, would depend in a considerable measure on the confidence it enjoys of all political parties. Therefore extraordinary care has got to be taken in appointing the Chief Election Commissioner who is supposed to deal with all the political parties having divergent views.

"There would be no room for such misguiding if the Chief Election Commissioner is appointed in consultation with the leader of the opposition in the Lok Sabha, or a member of House chosen by all opposition parties and the Chief Justice of India and/or of the Chairman of the Rajya Sabha" thus observed L.P. Singh, formerly Home Secretary, Union of India.

The procedure suggested above, no doubt would avoid the possible complaint that the party in power at the centre had been influenced by narrow considerations in choosing the Chairman of the Commission. At the earlier stages of the proceedings, the Constituent Assembly had thought of leaving it to each state to have its own Commission. It was only in 1949 that in order to ensure "uniformity of electoral procedure and practice in all the units" and "for the greatest safeguard for the purity of elections", it was decided that there should be an All India Election Commission with jurisdiction over both Union and State Elections.

Taking into consideration the present political scenario and the instability of the Government at the centre, as also the states due to *aaya ram and gaya ram,* and the unholy and unhealthy alliances between the diametrically opposed political parties, it is the crying need of the hour that the country, and hapless and helpless voters must have an Election Commission that may be amply and adequately empowered to hold the elections in a fair, impartial and fearless manner. The suggestions made by Mr. L.P. Singh for bringing reforms in the present electoral system are thought provoking and also worth taking serious note of.

REFERENCE

1. *Electoral Reform — Problems and Suggested Solutions* by L.P. Singh, Uppal Publication House, New Delhi.

3

CORRUPT PRACTICES

Free and fair election is the hallmark of a democratic and representative Government.

India is one of the largest democratic countries of the world and has witnessed eleven Lok Sabha elections. It has had equal number of Prime Ministers during the fifty years of our independence, the first was Pandit Jawaharlal Nehru and the latest is Shri Inder Kumar Gujral presently working as a caretaker Prime Minister after the dissolution of the 11th Lok Sabha. The Congress Party ruled the country for the largest period, but whenever the voter got extremely angry and unhappy with the style of functioning of the Government headed by the Congress Party, it gave to the country a new Government headed by a non-congress Prime Minister. This adequately shows the real power of the Indian voter. The number of Governments headed by the Prime Ministers belonging to different political parties is shown in the table on p. 12.

Shri Gulzari Lal Nanda became the acting Prime Minister of India, two times only for short intervals.

The change of Governments from time to time shows that the roots of democracy in our country are very deep, and the voter of this country by and large, is very mature and sensible and knows his duty very well.

But this is not enough. Something more is the dire need of the hour. All the political parties owe an onerous duty towards the country, so that the democratic process, works smoothly and peacefully. By putting candidates of shady character or with criminal back-ground, they make the job of the voter very difficult, in choosing the right type of person to represent his constituency. And the responsibility also lies on the shoulders of

Tenure	Name of the Prime Minister	Name of the Party
15th August 1947–27th May 1964	Jawaharlal Nehru	Indian National Congress
27th May 1964–9th June 1964	Gulzari Lal Nanda (Acting)	Indian National Congress
9th June 1964–11th June 1966	Lal Bahadur Shastri	Indian National Congress
11th June 1966–24th January 1966	Gulzari Lal Nanda (Acting)	Indian National Congress
24th January 1966–24th March 1977	Indira Gandhi	Indian National Congress
24th March 1977–28th July 1979	Morarji Desai	Janata Party
28th July 1979–14th January 1980	Ch. Charan Singh	Janata Party
14th January 1980–31st October 1984	Indira Gandhi	Indian National Congress
31st October 1984–1st December 1989	Rajiv Gandhi	Indian National Congress
2nd December 1989–10th November 1990	Vishwanath Pratap Singh	Janata Dal (National Front)
10th November 1990–21st June 1991	Chandra Shekhar	Break away group of National Front
21st June 1991–16 May 1996	P.V. Narasimha Rao	Indian National Congress
16 May 1996–1 June 1996	Atal Behari Vajpayee	Bhartiya Janata Party
1 June 1996–19 April 1997	H.D. Deve Gowda	Janata Dal (United Front)
20-4-1997–till date	Inder Kumar Gujral	Janata Dal (United Front)

those who man the election process of the country, i.e., the Election Commission. Happily, we have now a multi-member Election Commission, and all the three Election Commissioners, S/Sh. M.S. Gill, G.V.G. Krishamurthy and J.D. Lyndgo, have been working hard to conduct fair and free election in the country and have made some practical suggestions to improve the electoral process. It is on the recommendation of the Commission that the government has raised the limit of expenditure to Rs. 15 lakhs for Lok Sabha candidates and Rs. 5 lakhs for the MLAs.

The country indeed is passing through great crisis; all the institutions have been degenerating; the mafia has raised its ugly head; the politicians holding high positions have started indulging in corrupt practices. Scandals like Bofors, Fodder Scam,

Jain Hawala Scam, allotment of Petrol Pumps, allotments of houses etc., have come on surface in a very big way. The judicial institution is also under great strain and is facing attacks after attacks from many quarters. Let us not forget that a weak government at the centre will make every institution weak, and it certainly affects the very democratic fabric of the country.

The very success of democracy, therefore, depends on the due conduct of free and fair election so as to ensure the reflection of true popular will. For the accomplishment of this great task, strict legal provisions are also necessary for conducting impartial, independent, and free and fair elections in the country, so that undesirable practices are eliminated from the election arena. In India such undesirable practices are grouped as "Corrupt Practices." These are explained in Section 123 of the Representation of People Act, 1951. The whole section is reproduced at the end of this chapter for the benefit of the voters.

The Election Commission of India issued a Code of Conduct in 1984 after having a meeting with the representatives of all the political parties. The said code of conduct was designed to regulate the general conduct of political parties and candidates in the holding of election meetings, arranging processions, entry in the polling booths, and taking remedial measures to prevent booth capturing etc. The Election Commission derives its power under Article 324 of the Constitution, to superintend, direct, and control the election throughout the country.

A code of conduct is in fact a formalised set of healthy conventions for a democratic functioning. In Great Britain, conventions which have developed over a long period, have in practice the same force as legal enactments. Conventions, no doubt grow slowly and having been born out of experience, and developed through trial and error, acquire vitality only over a long period. It is high time that we made statutory enactments, and some of the most useful recommendations, by the Election Commission to the Government are made legally enforceable.

Misuse of Government machinery including the media and Doordarshan by the party in power also amounts to corrupt practices. The All India Radio, and Doordarshan should, therefore, function independently, impartially and without any discrimination whatsoever, for healthy and impartial elections. Ministers going to the constituencies for election campaigns should not be allowed to use government staff, conveyance or infray any other facility, which they are otherwise entitled to as a Minister. The Election Commission has to keep a constant vigil on such type of misuse by the men in power, which is in gross violation of Article 14 of the Constitution of India.

As a move in this direction, and providing equality of opportunity to all the recognised political parties, the least that needs to be done is to introduce an arrangement similar to one that exists in U.K. To quote from the report of a committee under the Chairmanship of Lord Houghton of Soverby (1975-76) on 'Financial Aid' to political parties, the arrangement is as follows:

"During a general election campaign the allocation of broadcasting time is decided by a Committee of party representatives and the broadcasting authorities. Apart from the election campaigns, the Committee decided each year on the party political broadcasting arrangements for the following years. The number and length of non-election broadcasts are related to votes received in the previous general election. In 1974, there were in total 18 television and 26 Radio non-election party political broadcasts.

No charge is made to the parties for any of their radio broadcast. For television the expenses to the parties need only small—generally not more then $100. If the parties had to buy advertising time on the I.T.V. television net work in the usual way, the cost would be of course very considerable."[1]

Before concluding, I am tempted to write an interesting incident, which perhaps may be quite relevant for the knowledge of the voters. After the unfortunate death of Pandit Jawaharlal Nehru, in the year 1964, Mrs. Vijaya Laxmi Pandit was the Congress candidate from Phoolpur Constituency. Indira Gandhi was then the Minister of Information and Broadcasting. Myself and Yashpal Kapoor were on the personal staff of Indira Gandhi. When Mrs. Gandhi went to Allahabad to campaign for her Phoophi, both of us though government officials, had accompanied her. Besides we attended to the official work, we also did the election work of Mrs. Vijaya Laxmi Pandit. We were treated on official duty for all the days we stayed at Allahabad. Whether it amounted to corrupt practices or not, I leave it to the countrymen and the Election Commission to make their own judgement. I have mentioned this incident only to appreciate all types of situations that do occur during the

[1]Electoral Reforms by L.P. Singh p. 51.

process of elections. There is indeed a thin line between the private work and official work as far as the personal staff of the Ministers is concerned.

Section 123 of the Representation of People Act, 1951 reads as under:

"*123-Corrupt practices: The following shall be deemed to be corrupt practices for the purpose of this act:-

(i) 'Bribery', that is to say:

A. Any gift, offer or promise by a candidate or his agent or by any other person with the consent of a candidate or his election agent of any gratification, to any person whomsoever, with the object, directly or indirectly of inducing:

(a) a person to stand or not to stand, as or to withdraw, or not to withdraw from being a candidate at an election, or

(b) an elector to vote or refrain from voting at an election, or as a reward to:

(i) a person for having so stood or not so stood, for having withdrawn or not having withdrawn from his candidature, or

(b) an elector for having voted or refrained from voting;

B. the receipt of, or agreement to receive, any gratification whether as a motive or a reward:

(a) by a person for standing or not standing as or for withdrawing or not withdrawing from being candidate; or

(b) by any person whomsoever for himself, or any other person for voting or refraining from voting, or inducing or attempting to induce any elector to vote or refrain from voting, or any candidate to withdraw or not to withdraw his candidature.

Explanation — for the purpose of this clause, the term 'gratification' is not restricted to pecuniary gratification, or gratifications estimable in money and it includes all forms of entertainment and all forms of employment for reward, but it does not include the payment of any expenses bonafide incurred at, or for the purpose of, any election, and duly entered in the account of election expenses referred to in the Section 78.

2. Undue influence, that is to say, any direct or indirect interference or attempt to interfere on the part of the candidate or his agent, or of any other person with the consent of the

candidate, or his election agent, with the free exercise of any electoral right:

Provided that:—

(a) without prejudice to the generality of the provisions of the clause any such person as is referred to therein who–

(i) threatens any candidate or any electoral, or any person and whom a candidate or any elector is interested, with injury of any kind including social obstruction and excommunication, or expulsion from any caste or community; or

(ii) induces or attempts to induce a candidate or an elector to believe that his or any person in whom he is interested, will become or will be rendered an object of divine displeasure or spiritual censure; shall be deemed to interfere with the free exercise of the electoral right of such candidate or elector within the meaning of this clause;

(b) a declaration of public policy, or promise of public action or the more exercise of a legal right without intent to interfere with an electoral right, shall not be deemed to be interference within the meaning of this clause;

(3) the appeal by a candidate or his agent or by any other person with the consent of a candidate or his election agent to vote or refrain from voting for any person on the ground of his religion, race, caste, community or language, or the use of, or appeal to religious symbols or the use of, or appeal to, national symbols, such as the national flag or the national emblem, for the furtherance of the prospects of the election of that candidate or prejudicially affecting the election of any candidate;

(Provided that no symbol allotted under this Act to a candidate shall be deemed to be a religious symbol or a national symbol for the purpose of this clause).

3-A. The promotion of, or attempt to promote, feelings of enmity or hatred between different classes of the citizens of India on grounds of religion, race, community or language by a candidate or his agent, or any other person with the consent of a candidate or his election agent for the furtherance of the prospects of the election of that candidate or for prejudicially affecting the election of any candidate;

(3-B) The propagation of the practice of the commission of State or its gratification by a candidate or his agent or any other person with the consent of the candidate or his election agent for the furtherance of the prospectus of the election of that candidate or for prejudicially affecting the election of any candidate.

Explanation: For the purpose of this clause, 'State and glorification" in relation to State shall have the meanings respectively assigned to them in the commission of Sati (Prevention) Act, 1987.

4. The publication by a candidate or his agent or by any other person with the consent of a candidate or his election agent, of any statement of fact which is false, and which he either believes to be false, or does not believe to be true, in relation to be the personal character or conduct of any candidate, being a statement reasonably calculated to prejudice the prospects of that candidate's election.
5. The hiring or procuring, whether on payment or otherwise, of any vehicle or vessel by a candidate or his agent or by any other person with the consent of a candidate or his election agent, or the use of such vehicle or vessel for the free coveyance of any elector (other than the candidate himself, the members of his family or his agent) to or from any polling station provided under Section 25 or a place fixed under sub Section 29 for the poll.

Provided that the hiring of a vehicle or vessel by an elector or by several electors at their joint costs for the purpose of conveying him or them to and from any such polling station or place fixed for the poll shall not be deemed to be a corrupt practice under this clause if the vehicle or vessel so hired is a vehicle or vessel not propelled by mechanical power;

Provided further that the use of any public transport vehicle or vessel or any tram-car or railway carriage by any elector at his own cost for the purpose of getting to or coming from any such polling station or place fixed for the poll shall not be deemed to be a corrupt practice under this clause.

Explanation: In this clause, the expression 'vehicle' means any vehicle used or capable of being used for the purpose of road transport, wherein propelled by mechanical power or otherwise and whether used for drawing other vehicles or otherwise.

6. The incurring or authorising of expenditure in contravention of Section 77.
7. The obtaining or procuring or abetting or attempting to obtain or procure by a candidate or his agent or by any other person with the consent of a candidate or his election agent, any assistance (other than the giving of vote) for the furtherance of the prospects of that candidates election, from any person in the service of the Government any belonging to any of the following classes, namely:

(a) Gazetted officers:
(b) Stipendiary judges and Magistrates;
(c) members of the armed forces of the Union;
(d) members of the policy forces;
(e) excise officers;
(f) revenue officers, other than village revenue officers known as lambardars, malguzars, patels, deshmukhs or by other name, whose duty is to correct land revenue and who are remunerated by a share of, or commission on the amount of land revenue collected by them but who do not discharge any police function; and
(g) such other class of persons in the service of the government as may be prescribed; 'Provided, that where any person in the service of the government and belonging to any of the classes aforesaid, in the discharge or purported discharge of his official duty, makes any arrangements or provides any facilities or does any other act or thing, for, to, or in relation to any candidate or his agent or any other person acting with the consent of the candidate or his election agent (wherein by reasons to the office held by the candidate or for any other reason), such arrangements, facilities or act or thing shall not be deemed to be assistance for the furtherance of the prospects of that candidate's election.

8. Booth capturing by a candidate or his agent, or other person:

Explanation: (1) In this Section the expression 'agent' includes an election agent, a polling agent and any person who is held to have acted as an agent in connection with the election with the consent of the candidate.

(2) for the purposes of clause (7), a person shall be deemed to assist in the furtherance of the prospects of a candidate's election if he acts as an election agent of that candidate.

(3) for the purpose of clause (7) not withstanding anything contained in any other law, the publication in the official gazette of the appointments, resignation, termination of service, dismissal or removal from service of a person in the service of the Central Government (including a person serving in connection with the administration of a Union Territory) or of a state Government shall be conclusive proof

(i) of such appointments, resignation, termination of service, dismissal or removal from service as the case may be, and

(ii) where the date of taking effect of such appointment, resignation, termination of service, dismissal or removal from service, as a case may be, is stated in such publication, also of the fact that such person was appointed with effect from the said date; or in the case of resignation, termination, of the service, dismissal or removal from service such person ceased to be in such service with effect from the said date.

4. For the purpose of clause (8) 'booth capturing' shall have the same meaning as in Section 135-A.

4

THE ELECTION SCENE: EMERGENCY PERIOD: 1975–77

The life breath of a healthy democracy lies in the proper, impartial and independent holding of free and fair elections without any pressure or coercion whatsoever from any quarter. By participating in the elections the Indian Voter, in a post independence era, had always felt a great sense of satisfaction. In fact there had always been a psychological feeling that he was the master of the destiny of his country through the proper use of his ballot. The Government that the voter chooses, is also expected to come upto the high hopes and expectations of the electorate. Whenever the elected Government faltered and lost the confidence of the people, the voter had shown his capacity to throw them out by the power of the ballot and not the bullet. This is the beauty of democratic process in our country.

The Congress Party headed by Pandit Jawaharlal Nehru ruled the country until his sad demise in the year, 1964. He continued to be the darling of the Indian people so long as he remained the Prime Minister. After his death, Shri Lal Bahadur Shastri was at the helm of affairs for a short period of 18 (eighteen) months as he died in a foreign land (Russia) mysteriously. After him, Smt. Indira Gandhi came on the political scene and she ruled the country in the first span till 1977, and was thrown out of power through ballot in the elections held in the year 1977 on account of emergency excesses and her dictatorial style of functioning. In the early period of seventies, she tried to ignore the democratic process and started acting in a dictatorial manner. In 1973 she superseded three seniormost Judges of the Supreme Court to tame the judiciary to her style of functioning.

Bogie of committed judiciary was then raised by Mohan Kumaramanglam, who was at that time in the Cabinet of Indira Gandhi. Era of supprsession of Supreme Court Judges, then started for the first time, when Indira Gandhi broke the long established convention of seniority on 25th April, 1973 by appointing Ajit Nath Ray, the next Chief Justice of India overriding his senior colleagues Justices Shelat, Hegde and Grover. The next suppression took place when Justice H.R. Khanna was replaced by Justice Beg in the year, 1977, possibily as a punishment for his dissent in habeas corpus petition. In 1996 efforts were again made to supersede Justice J.S. Verma. The Supreme Court Bar stood like a rock behind Justice Verma and saw to it that he was not superseded. Now that the term of Justice Verma is going to expire on 18th January, 1998, a malicous campaign by a disgruntled group of a few lawyers has been started against Justice M.M. Punchhi, who is the natural choice after Justice Verma's tenure expires as Chief Justice. Excerpts from the latest issue of India Today (January 5, 1998) are quite relevant and are reproduced:

> "After January 18 next, when Chief Justice of India, J.S. Verma retires who will occupy court No. 1 at the Supreme Court? Justice M.M. Punchhi, the seniormost Judge, shall fill the chair of the normal course of things, provided — as a 1993 Judgement of the apex Court goes — he is "considered fit to hold office, and proposal is initiated in advance by the Chief Justice of India". The trouble is Verma has not written a line yet to President, K.R. Narayanan on his choice of successor. The 1993 Judgement, delivered by a bench on which Verma was on the majority side, enjoins upon the Union Government to announce the name atleast a month in advance, by December 18, in this case. The Judgement also gives six weeks' time for the Government to process the Chief Justice's recommendation. To conform to his own judgement, Verma was required to recommend his successor latest by November 6. But there was no response from his office even as the Government's December 18 deadline for announcement went by such a long delay may point towards a doubt in the Chief Justice's mind about the "fitness" of his colleague . . . The confrontation can also be dangerous as it may lead to judicial chaos as in Pakistan, where the Chief Justice was pitted against his own

colleagues. Punchhi was a dissenter in the 1993 Judgement; so the bench is already split on the Chief Justice's right. Courts lose the moral high ground when they begin speaking on the key issues with a "forked tongue".

Prophetic words of Jaya Prakash Narayan

Jaya Prakash Narayan was the first person who could see the deterioration of almost all the institutions on account of autocratic and authoritarian approach of Indira Gandhi. Speaking at one of the meetings he told the audience that he was able to look ahead and see that "there is another 1942 in sight to change the course of history." J.P. was the main spirit behind the 1942 "do or die" movement, and was the first one to see gathering cloud on the political horizon. A year later Jaya Prakash Narayan was arrested on the midnight of 25th June, 1975, along with thousands of his followers and it was really 1942 all over again.

Indira Gandhi held Guilty of Corrupt Practices

A verdict against Indira Gandhi was handed down by Justice J.M.L. Sinha of Allahabad High Court. Indira Gandhi was found to have indulged in corrupt practices during the election compaign in her Rai Bareili constituency in 1971. In appeal, the Supreme Court, on 24th July, 1975 allowed her to continue as Prime Minister, but she was not given the right to vote as a Member of Lok Sabha till final disposal of her appeal.

Jaya Prakash Narayan had no personal ill will or animosity against Smt. Indira Gandhi, but he wanted her to step down in view of the Allahabad High Court Judgement. In a crucial public meeting on 25th June, 1975, at Ram Lila Ground, JP addressed the mammoth gathering. "A tall, lean, khadi clad JP, the darling of the masses, started his historic speech, in a soft, slow but clear and assertive voice. This was perhaps his last speech before the whole nation went into slavery for the next 21 months, a period of like of which was not experienced during the British regime even. The refusal to step down by Smt. Indira Gandhi, he claimed, was nothing but a mockery of democracy. In the same breath JP appreciated the stand taken by some Congress Members of Parliament including S/Shri Chandra Shekhar, Krishan Kant, Mohan Dharia, Mrs. T. Lakshmikantamma who had the courage and guts to tell Indira Gandhi to step down. JP in his speech even advised the army and police not to obey the orders which were wrong or illegal. He further reminded the army and the police that they were dutybound to defend not only the country and the people,but also the constitution.

Midnight Arrests: After the crucial public meeting, Jaya Prakash went back to his place of residence at Gandhi Peace Foundation at Rouse Avenue.The Government was obviously shaken and perturbed at the tremendous success of the public meeting addressed by Lok Nayak and many other prominent leaders. Instructions had already been issued to all the police stations. Around 2 A.M. at night Jaya Prakash Narain was woken up by one of his close aides and told that the police had come to arrest him. He was mildly surprised as he had not expected that Mrs. Indira Gandhi would be that mean. The aides of Jaya Prakash Narain informed some congress members of Parliament including Chander Shekhar, Krishan Kant, Ram Dhan and Mohan Dharia who immediately rushed to Shri Jaya Prakash Narain's Place. They accompanied Shri Jaya Prakash Narain to the Parliament Police Station. Before leaving the place, Shri Jaya Prakash Narain remarked "Vinash Kale, Virprit Buddhi".

The Lok Nayak rightly saw the beginning of the subversion of Indian Democracy and the dawn of authoritarianism and dictatorship.

A veteran freedom fighter linked the events of June 25 and 26, 1975 to the Pre-Dawn swoop on Mahatma Gandhi and other important leaders following the Quit India Movement launched on August 9, 1942.

The Government headed by Smt. Indira Gandhi had thus completely shaken the faith of the people of India who had brought her to power with a thumping majority through the use of their ballot, a valuable vote. This was indeed a great betrayal of the mandate of the countrymen in her favour. Since the country is faced with another election, likely to be held in the first week of March, 1998, it would be appropriate to mention the Chronological events of the dark days of the emergency, which may prove to be an eye opener while casting the sacred vote to the right person and the right party.

12th June 1975

Allahabad High Court holds Mrs.Indira Gandhi guilty of corrupt practices in her election campaign as a Member of Parliament.

22nd June, 1975

Janata Front launched a frontal attack and demanded the resignation of Smt. Indira Gandhi as Prime Minister.

25th June, 1975

A historic public meeting was held at the Ram Lila Grounds, demanding the resignation of Mrs. Indira Gandhi. To spearhead the nation-wide compaign against the dictatorial design of Mrs. Indira Gandhi and her henchmen, Lok Sangarsh Samiti was formed.

Under the instructions of the Prime Minister, the Delhi Police swung into action and arrested the Prominent Leaders at midnight, when they were asleep at their residence.

President declared proclamation of Emergency under duress by signing the said draft Emergency proclamation.

June 26, 1975

The Prime Minister of India, Smt. Indira Gandhi addressed the Indian people, and says that the President has declared emergency in the country, "There is nothing to panic about.".

June 27, 1975

V.C. Shukla replaces I.K. Gujral from I & B Ministry as he (Gujral) refused to toe the line of Sanjay Gandhi. Censorship imposed, and severe restrictions imposed on the foreign press.

June 30, 1975

President passes ordinance amending Misa (Maintenance of Internal Security Act) whereby no ground need to be given for arrest made under it.

July 4, 1975

The centre bans the Anand Marg, R.S.S, Jamat-i-Islami and Naxalite Groups.

July 23, 1975

Lok Sabha appproves Emergency by a majority vote of 336 against 56.

August 4, 1975

Government introduces a Bill to implement in retrospect, the Allahabad High Court Judgement. It provided that any person disqualified on the basis of corrupt electoral practices would have the right to appeal to the President, who will have the final say after consulting the Election Commission. Lok Sabha passes the bill the next day.

August 7, 1975

At 11 A.M. the government introduced the Constitution (40th Amendment) Bill which provided authority, beyond the scope of any court to deal with the election of the President, Vice-President, Prime Minister and the Speaker of the Lok Sabha. It makes doubly sure that no election petition ever affects Indira Gandhi, the then Prime Minister of India. After 11.08 A.M. the Government moves the Bill for consideration, which is passed at 1.50 P.M. after clause by clause discussion and the required three readings.

August 8, 1975

The State Legislatures where the Congress had a majority are summoned and the requisite ratification secured on August 9, 1975.

August 10, 1975

The President gives his assent to the Bill. The next day the Supreme Court was to hear Indira Gandhi's appeal. It was ratractively applied from June 29, 1975.

October 9, 1975

The néws circuit of reuters is cut for putting out stories 'in violation' of censorship rules.

November 7, 1975

Based on the new Election Laws (Amendment) Act, 1975 a Constitution Bench of the Supreme Court unanimously upholds the election of Indira Gandhi to the Lok Sabha from Rae Bareily.

July 1976

The sterilisation drive was stepped up and gained momentum a month later, resulting in 240 incidents of violence on account of resistance to forced sterilisation.

January 18, 1977

Mrs. Indira Gandhi dissolves the Lok Sabha, elections announced.

January 20, 1977

Emergency is relaxed and instructions rushed to State Governments to release detenus.

February 11, 1977

President Fakhruddin Ali Ahmed dies.

March 16 to 20, 1977

Polls held throughout the country.

March 24, 1977

Moraji Desai sworn in as Prime Minister. Non-Congress Government came in power, for the first time, at the Centre.

The Power of the Ballot

We have, therefore, noticed that the period of 1975 to 1977, had been a period of gloom, darkness, authoritarianism, dictatorship and the rule of the jungle. The voters who had pinned their hopes, aspirations, and the confidence in the Congress Party and gave them, as usual a decisive mandate, were thoroughly betrayed. Instead of getting good governance, they got untold miseries, and great hardships; their fundamental rights, were suspended, thousands of innocent men, women and the young boys, and girls were put behind the bars without knowing the hows and whys of their arrest; even the President of India was forced to declare internal emergency, and the courts were functioning under great strain and political directions. The worst that could have happened, had happened during the dark days of emergency, and the people of India bravely, boldly and in a dignified manner put up with all these miseries and hardships. But the moment the opportunity came, they made the appropriate use of their vote at the elections and brought a silent, peaceful and yet a decisive total revolution by overthrowing the cruel government through the power of "the ballot" and not the bullet.

The Indian voter today again is at cross roads, the representatives whom they sent to the Parliament have unfortunately failed to deliver goods, and have not been able to provide a stable Government; in less than two years period three Governments have changed hands, and have ultimately come to the 'Peoples' Court to seek a fresh mandate. The voter certainly is in a great dilemma, but still we have to find an answer and make every possible effort in the right direction to choose a right representative to get a right Government — stable and able.

In the last chapter we have tried to find the answer through the wisdom of mature, impartial and independent thinkers belonging to all walks of life. But before we conclude, the following appeal made by Shri Jaya Prakash Narain to the voters of the country during the elections in the 1977, seem to be very relevant even today, as it brought the desired result in choosing a right Government after the black period of emergency.

JP's Appeal to Countrymen

Mr. Jayaprakash Narayan has made the following appeal to the people of India:

> In the name of all those who struggled for our country's freedom, I appeal to each of you: Free India, defeat the dictators.
>
> This is the last chance, if you falter, 19 months of tyranny shall become 19 years of terror.
>
> Our goal is progress with Justice.

Freedom is the first requisite to achieve this goal. We have seen during the last 19 months how, when freedom is crushed, the poor, the workers are intimidated to slave for enriching a small coterie at the top. When freedom is lost, all is lost.

We want our officials and our elected representatives to be accountable to our people.

Freedom alone can ensure that they are so. How will the rulers are accountable if the judiciary is robbed of all effectiveness? How can you end corruption if you cannot even talk or write about it? How can we have accountability if power is exercised by backroom operators who do not even hold office?

The terror of the black 19 months, herding hundreds of thousands into jails, the tortures inflicted on them, the untold sufferings of their families, mutiliating laws so that a citizen does not even have the right of life, illicit as well as illegal extortions, destroying homes of the poor — these are not chance happenings, they are what dictatorship is about.

None of these attrocities could have happened in a free society. If you could have talked about them, if you could have met and organised to resist them, if the press could have written about them, an aroused and informed public opinion would have set its face against the oppressors.

Contrast the black 19 months with the relative freedom of the last two months. The very rulers who were asserting that the people do not want elections, who talked of gains of Emergency, those very rulers are today seeking alibis for that action and are compelled to offer apologies. Just mited freedom at that has forced them to once again take account of the people.

Do you want the irresponsibility, the brutality of the 19th months to return? Do you want your 30,000 brothers and sisters who have still not been released, to continue in prison indefinitely? Do you want the set up to continue in which each of you can be arrested without explanation, in which you can be held indefinitely without trial, in which the rulers are free to do what they will with you — and no one, not even your familities will know what is happening?

And my brothers and sisters in the minority communities must remember that Fundamental Rignts and a free and open society are even more important for them than for the majority. In addition to restoring Fundamental Rights and the rule of law, the Janata Party will establish a Civil Rights Commission to specifically protect the interests of minorities. Similarly, nothing will benefit the poor in general and the minorities in particular as much as the right to work as a Fundamental Right.

Many efforts have been made to hoodwink you and to distract you. Destabilisers who are responsible for splitting up all institutions in this country have talked of stability. They have tried to inflame communal passions, to frighten minorities, even to capitalise on Bapu's murder. They have tried to scare you with stories of violence of external and internal threats. They have issued sham apologies. They have tried to pass the blame for their dastardly deeds to officials, even to us who were in jails. They have tried to bribe you with last minute concessions. They have tried to mislead you with lies about the Janata Party's programme.

Do not let any of these mislead you. Be like Arjuna and like him do no let your eye wander from the central issue: Freedom or slavery, democracy or dynastic dictatorship.

Remember that the ruling party still swears by the black laws and amendments that it used as the basis of its dictatorship. It will use them ruthlessly, should it get another chance. Its leaders have clearly said that there is no room for differences of opinion in India that they are the country. That far from being unhappy, the hundreds of thousands who were jailed should be grateful that they were not shot to death.

The Janata Party, by contrast, is pledged to restore a free and open society. It is pledged to repealing the black laws and amendments. The very process by which it will be acquiring power — through the current struggle for freedom, through your support for the cause of freedom — will guarantee that it will fulfill its pledge.

Remember that each seat counts and that for each seat each and every vote counts. Translate the enthusiasm we have witnessed during the last few weeks into votes for the Janata Party.

Defeat the dictators. We can then build a free and Gandhian India.

Vote for Janata Party
Vote for power to people
Vote for the "Man carrying the Plough".

5

THE ELECTION SCENE: POST EMERGENCY PERIOD 1977–1997

After the 1977 General Election, the Janata Party came into power with Morarji Desai, as the next Prime Minister of India. Soon after coming into power, a politics of vengeance had started. To try Shrimati Indira Gandhi, and punish her was the first item on their agenda. Shah Commission, under the chairmanship of Justice J.C. Shah was appointed to go into the atrocities committed during emergency. The government media, including the All India Radio went on highlighting the proceedings of the Shah Commission and a full fledged hate campaign had started against Indira Gandhi and the prominent persons who worked overzealously during emergency.

The voter soon got disappointed and felt completely betrayed. They had voted out Indira Gandhi for her authoritarian and dictatorial behaviour, with the fervent hope that under JP's leadership they would get a government that works, and looks after the burning problems of the millions of weak and meek. Their hopes and aspirations were soon shattered to pieces, and they felt cheated and humbled to the maximum extent. Sharp differences soon came to surface between Ch. Charan Singh and Morarji Desai. Morarji Desai wanted to go slow on Indira Gandhi, but Ch. Charan Singh was in great haste to send her to jail. JP wanted to interfere, and give his wise counsel, but he was completely ignored, and sidelined. There was complete confusion and disillusionment among the people, who rightly felt that instead of looking into the long standing problems of the country and the poor people the government was concentrating on settling their personal scores with Indira Gandhi and her close associates. The net result was that the Janata Government was torn into pieces and Morarji Desai had to tender his resignation. After the fall of Morarji Desai's Government, Indira Gandhi played her cards very well, and allowed Ch. Charan Singh to form the Government with the outside support of Congress. Because of his life's ambition to become Prime Minister and adorn the highest seat of power, he was fully trapped and immediately after he took oath as Prime Minister, Mrs. Gandhi said her job was over. And soon after she withdrew her support, and finished Ch. Charan Singh for ever. He is perhaps the only Prime Minister, who could not attend the Parliament as a Prime Minister even for a single day. Without seeking the vote of confidence, he tendered his resignation.

The country was again pushed into fresh Lok Sabha Elections, and the voters were again put to great test. They threw out Indira Gandhi to have a good, stable and democratic Government, but their hopes were belied, as the new government (Janata Government) also miserably failed to deliver the goods. Even they completely ignored their own leader Jayaprakash Narayan, who was the main force behind their victory. In the 1980 Lok Sabha Elections, the voters were left with no other choice, but to bring back Indira Gandhi into power, and she thus got atonement for the sins she had committed during emergency. It goes without saying that it was the leadership which failed the democratic process, and not the voter who always tried to give the mandate as per the circumstances demanded them to use their right of ballot in a rightful manner as far as possible. Kudos to the Indian voter. He has always tried to tilt towards the lesser evil.

The result was that the Congress Party under the leadership of Indira Gandhi again came in power in the 1980 Lok Sabha Elections. But the tragic end of Indira Gandhi came in the year 1984, when she was killed at her own residence with a dozen of bullets pierced into her body. After the untimely death of Mrs. Gandhi, Rajiv Gandhi was given an oath of the Prime Minister, without even being formally elected as the leader of the Parliamentary Party. To start with his performance was quite appreciable, and he was described among the general masses as 'Mr. Clean'. But sometime later, his style of functioning changed dramatically, may be due to the ill-advice of the coterie around him. Later on he strained his relations with the President, who went out of the way to administer him an oath of the office of the Prime Minister. He was also involved in the Bofors Controversy on account of which V.P. Singh had to part company and had to form Jan Morcha, after having been expelled from the Congress. On 24th March, 1986 the Indian Government signed a contract with A.B. Bofors to buy 400 field howitzers (FH 77) and ammunition worth over Rs. 1,700 crore, after Bofors gave an assurance that there were no middlemen in the deal. And on April 16, 1987, Swedish Radio reported that Bofors paid bribes to Indian politicians and key defence figures to win the contract. On 20th April 1987, Rajiv Gandhi denied the charge on the Floor of the House; on 6th August 1987, the government appointed Joint Parliamentary Committee of 30 Members of Parliament to identify the recipients of the 64 crore commission paid by Bofors. But the opposition boycotted the committee under protest.

V.P. Singh spearheaded the move to demand the resignation of Rajiv Gandhi. Addressing a public meeting, V.P. Singh said that even though the Press, the Parliament, and the urban Indians needed to be reminded continuously about the importance of the Bofors issue, his visits elsewhere in India convinced him that the people are aware of the corruption and bribery rampant in Mr. Rajiv Gandhi's Government and his availability in the Bofors scandal.

Addressing the audience Mr. Dandvate said, that in the first instance Rajiv Gandhi told that no commission was paid. When it was proved otherwise he told that no Indians were paid, and when that statement was also proved incorrect, he replied that no Indians concerned with the government were paid. And ultimately when the "Hindu" revealed the names, Mr. Rajiv Gandhi said, "if the commissions were paid for a good cause, what is wrong in accepting it."

When the C.A.G. (Comptroller and Auditor-General) Report was being attacked by the Congress members of parliament, leaders of different political parties (S/Shri Dipen Ghosh–CPIM, P. Upendra–TDP, M.S. Gurupad Swamy–JD, L.K. Advani–BJP, Gurudas Gupta–CPI, Aladi Anuna–AIADMK, Dr. Nagen Saikia–AGP, T.R. Babu–DMK and Chitta Basu–FB), issued a statement saying that they wanted PM's resignation and not-discussion. They further said, " During the past few years, one by one every constitutional institution — Parliament, Presidency, Judiciary, Governor, Election Commission etc. — is being devalued and denigrated. Now a frontal assault has been mounted on yet another constitutional institution–C &

A.G . . . We cannot be a party to a debate prompted by such malafide intentions. The Comptroller and Auditor General's Report is a conclusive finding on the l'affaire Bofors. It calls for follow up action and not discussion. And the only logical follow-up to such a report in a democracy is that Prime Minister Rajiv Gandhi should resign."

For the first time in the history of Parliament, as many as 106 members of Parliament tendered their resignation in protest. The resignation en masse by the opposition MPs was the result of the insults that Rajiv Gandhi heaped on them. The JPC which went into the Bofors Gun Deal, was purely made a purely Congress(I) show. The probe into the West German submarine contract was entrusted to the Defence Secretary. The PAC chairmanship was taken away from the opposition and the Congress (1) did not mind when the opposition members resigned from all the Parliamentary Committees. The MPs who had resigned represented more than 100 million in the country (one Lok Sabha constituency has a population of eight to 10 lakh voters), thus observed Kuldeep Nayar.*

Ultimately the Lok Sabha was dissolved prematurely in spite of the fact that it had a massive mandate. After the dastardly murder of Indira Gandhi on 31st October 1984, Rajiv Gandhi remained in power as Prime Minister until 1st December 1989. The term of the eighth Lok Sabha was to expire on 14th January, 1990, but the general elections were held on 22, 24 and 26th November 1989 because of the dissolution of the Lok Sabha prematurely.

It is a well-known fact that the Bofors issue was highlighted during the election campaign, throughout the country. The election scene in 1989 was marked by widespread violence. There were hundreds of poll clashes and indiscriminate use of lathis, guns, daggers and bombs. Even in violation of the instructions issued by the election commission, most of the political parties had shown scant regard for the recommendation and guidelines of the Election Commission. 'To cite only a few examples, the Congress (1) list (for the Lok Sabha and Assembly elections in 1989) included one candidate who had five criminal cases pending against him, another candidate who had been named in more than 30 murder cases, still another candidate who had been detained for organising a bomb attack, and a fourth one charged by the CBI of swindling cooperative funds. Lists of some of the other parties did not lag far behind.'

All the anti-Congress parties joined together, and defeated the Congress (1) in the 1989 elections. The political parties with different ideologies, i.e., B.J.P, CPI (M) came together and supported the government headed by the National Front, with V.P. Singh as the Prime Minister. From day one, after V.P. Singh took over as the Prime Minister, he had been facing difficulties after difficulties from different constituents. Chandra Shekhar from the very beginning publicly declared that V.P. Singh was not his leader. Devi Lal used to threaten him that it was he who made him the Prime Minister. BJP had agreed to give him only conditional support. Therefore most of time of V.P. Singh was spent in cajoling and arranging the tables of the different constituents and nothing useful could be done for the people who had brought them to power. To keep himself in perpetual seat of power, V.P. Singh dug out the Mandal Report gathering dust on the government shelves and declared its implementation to please a particular set of people. So many lives of young students were lost, but he stuck to his guns even in the face of strong resistance from many quarters. In reply to the Mandal issue the BJP raised the Ayodhya issue to gain sympathy and attract the attention of a particular set of vote bank. Bajpayee is on record to say that 'Tumne Mandal kiya to hamne kamandal kiya.'

Thus this was the beginning of the era of the caste and class war. People of different schools of thought got very much disgusted and again the atmosphere of chaos and confusion came to the surface. L.K. Advani took out a 'rath' to reach Ayodhya, but as soon as he entered Bihar he was arrested by Laloo Prasad Yadav. BJP was then left with no other alternative than to withdrew its support to the V.P. Singh Govt. And that was thus the end of the National Front Government, headed by Shri V.P. Singh.

Due to the infighting of constituents of different political parties, the biggest sufferer and the victim were the people, who voted them to power with the earnest hope that they would govern the country with efficiency and would bring stability in the country but alas it could not happen.

After the fall of V.P. Singh Govt. Chandra Shekhar came into power. But he could not stay any longer as the Congress headed by Rajiv Gandhi withdrew the support, in gross violation of the assurance given to the then President, Shri R. Venkataraman that they would not withdraw the support for atleast one year. So the Ninth Lok Sabha did not serve its full term and the house was dissolved on 12th March 1991, when Chandra Shekhar tendered his resignation from the office of Prime Minister. Chandra Shekhar continued as care taker Prime Minister till 21st June 1991, when P.V. Narasimha Rao took over as the next Prime Minister after the results of the 10th Lok Sabha elections were declared. Happily the government headed by Narasimha Rao completed its full term, and he continued as such till 16th May 1996. The term of tenth Lok Sabha was upto 8th July 1996. The general elections to the eleventh Lok Sabha were held on 27th April 1996. The term of Narasimha Rao was full of scandals and scams, and the people again were utterly disgusted from the Congress misrule. Criminalisation of politics was at its peak during the tenure of Narasimha Rao. The PIL (Public Interest Litigation) was the order of the day since almost all the institutions failed to work and look into the burning problems of the people.

In the 11th Lok Sabha Elections the people gave a fractured mandate and made it very difficult for any party to form the government. BJP being the largest party, got the first opportunity to form the government. So Atal Bihari Vajpayee was administered the oath of Prime Minister on 16th May 1996. Since he could not prove his majority he tendered his resignation. And as per normal practice, the President asked Mr. Vajpayee to continue as care taker Prime Minister till the new government was formed.

The people who gave the fractured mandate had been silently watching these political acrobats. All the other parties, including the Congress which was the second largest party could not find out a person who could be named as the next Prime Minister. Politics of 'Joar toar' (expediency) had been started with the soul aim of keeping communal forces out of power. But from among the elected representatives, they could not agree to any one name. Ultimately, a farmer from Karnataka who was then the Chief Minister of the State could be brought around to adorn the highest office. Neither was he the Member of Parliament, nor was he willing in the first instance to accept the offer. But the 13 parties conclave persuaded him to accept the office of the Prime Minister. He was thus administered the oath of the office of Prime Minister on 1st June 1996. Therefore the people were given a Prime Minister, whom they never elected. This name could come on surface, after the formation of the United front. The topmost names for this office were, V.P. Singh, Jyoti Basu, G.K. Moopanaar, Ram Krishna Hegde and Mr. Laloo Prasad Yadav. H.D. Deve Gowda was thus the last choice of the United Front, which was forced on the electorate most undemocratically and against all norms and values cherished by our forefathers.

The marriage of convenience could not last long on account of infighting and mud slinging among the various constituents. The Congress party which had offered support from outside, also felt completely ignored and ultimately pulled down government headed by H. D. Deve Gowda. The Parliament debates are a witness to the humiliations and condemnations inflicted upon Deve Gowda in person, and the National Front Government in general, while bringing a no confidence motion against the government. Thus after a span of 11 months, the government headed by H.D. Deve Gowda met its doom and lost the vote of confidence on the floor of the House.

Old Wine in New Bottle

The Congress Party, second largest with 140 members or so was the deciding factor, whether to seek fresh electi ns or form a government to avoid election. After having meetings of the working committee and serious deliberations, the Congress Party headed by Sita Ram Kesri finally came to the conclusion, that the fresh elections should be avoided. They then pin pointed a pliable person, I.K. Gujral, who was the Foreign Minister in Deve Gowda's Govt. and told the United Front leaders, that the Congress could give outside support, if Shri I.K. Gujral was made the Prime Minister. Without going into detail, it is sufficient to mention here, that the name of I.K Gujral was cleared by the United Front. The Congress Party thus addressed a letter to the President offering outside support to the United Front, and the President Shri K.R. Narayanan administered an oath of office of the Prime Minister to Shri I.K. Gujral. The Congress Party had cordial relations with I.K. Gujral and went on smoothly for some time.

Jain Commission Report

The dramatic release of Interim report of Jain Commission alleging the hand of DMK in the assassination of Rajiv Gandhi, turned the tables. Sita Ram Kesri, the Congress President, demanded the head of three DMK Ministers, who were in the Gujral Government but the Gujral Government firmly decided not to oblige the Congress Party. The government, in turn asked the Congress Party to first have discussion on the report before any decision was taken to drop those ministers. Ultimately, the Congress Party withdrew its support from the Gujral Government and sent a letter of withdrawal of support from the government. The result was, that the 11th Lok Sabha also came to an end within less than two years of existence, and the country is once again pushed into elections for a fresh mandate by the Indian voter.

Before we end this chapter, let us have quick look of the failed coalition that took place in the year 1997.

Government fell like nine pins as two Prime Ministers and Chief Ministers in three states could not tame political ambitions in 1997 and uncertainty reigned supreme.

Scams and marriage of convenience dictated political activities in the 50th year of independence, which nonetheless saw a dalit become the country's President. With predictions of another hung Parliament in the offing, the run up to the ballot sees strange alliances taking shape in a scramble for the Lok Sabha. (This writer most respectfully differs from the views expressed by Sudha Passi in Economic Times of 29th December 1997, and is quite optimistic that one major political party will be able to form the government with the help of its allies.

Here is a chronology of political events in 1997.

January 9, 1997: Congress (I) leaders N.D. Tiwari and Arjun Singh return to Congress (I).

February 10: The Shiromani Akali Dal ally BJP sweeps assembly elections in Punjab with 90 seats in the 117 member house.

March 12: Cabinet extends President's rule in UP.

March 18: Former Union Minister Kalpnath Rai jailed for ten years for harbouring Dawood Ibrahim aides.

March 21: Ms. Mayawati becomes Uttar Pradesh's Chief Minister under a six month power sharing formula between the BJP and BSP.

March 30: Congress (I) Sita Ram Kesri withdraws support to Mr. Deve Gowda's United Front Government.

April 20: Mr. I.K. Gujral sworn in as Prime Minister of the UF Government.

May 8: Mrs. Sonia Gandhi enrols as Primary Congress (I) member.

May 29: Mr. Rajesh Pilot and Sharad Pawar file papers to contest the Congress (I) Presidential Polls, while Sharad Yadav enters fray for the top post in Janata Dal.

June 13: Mr. Sita Ram Kesri elected President of the Congress (I) in polls, the first in 14 years.

June 18: Bihar Governor A.R. Kidwai sanctions prosecution of Chief Minister Laloo Prasad Yadav in fodder scam while Mr. Gujral seeks resignation of two union Ministers accused in the scam.

July 7: Sharad Yadav elected the Janata Dal President.

July 25: Mr. K.R. Narayanan becomes the first dalit President of India.

July 26: Laloo Prasad resigns and instals Rabri Devi Chief Minister.

August 14: Parliament re-enacts 'freedom at midnight'.

August 16: Mr Krishan Kant elected Vice-President.

August 26: Parliament begins special four day session to discuss development strategy for next century.

August 28: Election Commission bars convicts from contesting polls notwithstanding a pending appeal in a higher court.

Jain Commission submits its 17-volume interim report.

August 29: The Delhi High Court cancels allotment of petrol pumps by Mr. Satish Sharma under Minister's discretionary powers.

September 12: The High Court directs Narasimha Rao and 18 others to face trial in JMM bribery case.

September 21: Kalyan Singh assumes charge as Chief Minister, Uttar Pradesh.

October 20: BSP withdraws support to Kalyan Singh government, but he succeeds to prove his majority in Vidhan Sabha.

October 23: The Central Government forced to backtrack on central rule in Uttar Pradesh after the President asks it to reconsider its decision.

November 16: Press leaks of Jain Commission Report triggers political upheaval as the Congress (1) seeks the ouster of DMK Ministers.

November 28: Mr. Gujral submits resignation to President.

December 4: President dissolves 11th Lok Sabha.

December 11: Laloo Prasad secures bail and decides to form an alternative secular front with Congress (I), SP and BSP.

December 12: Congress (I) leaders Krishna Sahi and Jagannath Mishra quit party.

December 15: Orissa JD splits with 29 members forming Biju Janata Dal.

December 25: Four former congress (I) ministers join the BJP while the Congress (I) expels rebel leader Mamata Bannerji.

December 26: Gujarat Assembly dissolved after split in Mr. Vaghela's RJP and political uncertainty.

December 30: Sonia Gandhi declares that she would actively campaign for congress in the Lok Sabha Elections — Jubilations in the Congress circles.

6

BALLOTING FARCE*

Numerically induced catastrophe has caused premature demise of the Eleventh Lok Sabha. It could be averted. But due to lack of maturity, vision, direction and perception of our political masters who have been entrusted with the destiny of our nation, the wheel of governance has been brought to a grinding halt. As ordained by the presidential command a renewed exercise has to be made to constitute the Twelfth Lok Sabha before March 15, 1998. Till the next Lok Sabha comes into existence, there would be lame duck executive dispensation under the stewardship of the outgoing Prime Minister who owes no accountability to anyone during the interregnum. Governance is a continuous process and slipshod governance, vacuum or voidness therein can be disastrous, perilous and accursed phenomenon.

The psyche of Indian voter has very seriously been bruised as he is feeling woefully disenchanted with prevailing dismal political scenario, rigid, unwholesome, unsound and anti-poor electoral system and degeneration of socio, economical and cultural ethos. He is feeling himself irrelevant and directionless as if he has lost his very indentity. He is groping into darkness to find meaningful remedies to the maladies afflicted upon him by political pestilents, bandtis and predators. The word politics is considered a dirty and detestable word by the voter. He has developed indifference and insensitivity to often orchestrated fictive rhetoric that he is the ultimate sovereign.

He understands the deceitful, dishonest, selfish intentions and tantrums of political tradesman and cannot be pampered anymore and refuses to be a playful thing. He has become sick

* Avtar Singh Sohal, Advocate, Supreme Court of India.

of witnessing grostesque and farcical balloting melodrama. There is nothing to enthuse or inspire him to trust the vainglorious and grandiloquent promises trumpted with a view to once again usurp his valuable right of franchise. His past, trackrecord is appalling. He is like a political Santa Claus feigning to be epitome of piety, compassion, honesty, truthfulness and sincerity. It is mirage and his bag is empty and he does not believe in quid pro-quo, nor he has got anything to offer in return.

He came earlier also, several times like the present one and begged for bounty of ballot and voter though did not believe his false promises yet obliged him. Everytime when he comes he shamefacedly flaunts plums afresh without rendering past account and brazenly forges some alibi to cheat the voter. The voter is no more gullible and he knows his tricks, yet, but once again will oblige him by giving his ballot in dole out of generosity and in vain and fond hope that he might one day try to become credible and trustworthy. The vote seeker is conscious, that the voter has reservoir of endurance which he can exploit ad inifinitum. But this reservoir can dry up. The judgement day is not too far. People are waiting for crusador, messiah another JP to lead them to usher in new era where even the last man in the street feels relevant, secured economically, socially, and culturally. True democracy can only thrive and survive if the lowest of the lowly is empowered. It may sound utopian but this is aspiration of the people and goal of our constitution.

The Indian society today stands horizontally dichotomised into two broad segments which can be described as upper and lower strata, elitists and commoners or haves and have nots. In our constitutional scheme whose aim is welfare state and classless society, this schism should be not acceptable. But is it a reality. Some well meaning social scientists and thinkers should research the wide ranging subject. I am not dilating herein upon diverse contours of the malaise due to constraint of space. Nevertheless, I feel adverting to the electoral participation by both the classes. In theory every adult citizen irrespective of his social status whether one is belonging to one class or other has similar right of franchise. It is common knowledge that the user of that right is invariably not identical in both the cases. Elitist voter shirks from standing and waiting in queue alongwith the have nots. He has learnt to jump the queue. To him this balloting exercise is fruitless, unprofitable embarrassing exercise. He has scant regard to his sacred and social duty cast upon him by virtue of being citizen of country to participate in the task of electing a representative governing machinery. He moves out of cocoon only when he tastes power himself. He tries to wield power to promote his socio-economical and other interests. His motivation is never service of people and political pursuits are founded on personal interests. The higher strata people whether they directly wield the reins of power or not always have excess, to corridors of power and think themselves to have birth-right to enjoy executive largesse.

The less privileged voter treats it a sacrosanct task of choosing legislators. His participation terminates with the marking of his ballot. He cannot muster courage himself to enter into electoral fray due to lack of requisite wherewithal (financial, physical and manipulative) resources, which his counterpart is privileged to possess. Recent enhancement of poll expenses impliedly establishes the thesis that for parliamentary election one must have resources of garnering this staggering sum. It means electoral game is for privileged affluent persons and not for a have not, howsoever, sincere, devoted and well meaning social activist he may be. It is sad commentary on our antipoor electoral mechanism which prevents right type of person from joining the legislative team to administer the country in the best interests of all the sections of the society. Inevitable consequences of all that his choice is strait jacketed. His own class is kept away and he is per force compelled to cast his vote in favour of alien contestant who has no nexus with his class. The balloting farce is of no consequence to a man in the street. Neither he can contest, nor his class is represented nor he has excess to corridors of power. He has to run from pillar to post for succour as if he is son of a lessor God.

A serious debate should be initiated at national level. We must address to the malfunctioning of our electoral mechanism and remedial measures have to be found. Till we empower the last man in the street, the democracy will remain a meaningless and farcical and sham system.

Adverting to the recently demised Lok Sabha, it could be saved and it ought to have been allowed to live normal life of five years. The electorate voted in favour of five hundred and forty four persons with fond hope that they would as per the constitutional mandate transact business of governance for five years and did not expect that they would stymie the house by not allowing themselves to be extricated from the vortex of number game. The responsible legislators ought to have realised that they were voted in to govern and not to fight. A common man understands that the concept of coalition has utterly failed and there is no chance in forseable future to give majority to a particular party. In these circumstances the members of Lok Sabha ought to have crossed party lines and evolved a viable alternative to ensure uninterrupted and unhindered process of administering the country. What was the difficulty of leaving the selection of the leader to the Lok Sabha itself? It could be done by treating the house as electroal college and by secret single transferable vote elected the Prime Minister who in turn could have selected efficient council of ministers. But it was not to be. They have disappointed the electorates and have burdened the exchequer with heavy unbearable electoral expenses. They ought to have coolly and dispassionately realised that what is guarantee that next parliament would not be hung. There appears no bright chance to be optimistic that the next Lok Sabha would not be hung.

I am an eligible voter. I shall surely once again mark the ballot to the best of my judgement despite lot of odds and discomfiture. Though I do not have faith in any political outfit yet once again, I will entertain bright and diamond hope that the next Lok Sabha will live normal life.

7

"POLLS ARE OFTEN FAKE"*

They amount to direct interference with the free choice of voters — and democracy

To be truly democratic, any democracy must ensure the election of representatives by free choice of voters. It is axiomatic, therefore, that the voters are allowed to exercise the choice of their independent will, uninfluenced by others. For this reason, the Election Code in India lays down that 24 hours before voters go to the polling stations — and during the polling days — all propaganda and campaigning should stop. This enables voters to make their choice in a cool and peaceful atmosphere.

It is a known phenomenon all over the world that the so-called pre-poll survey and exit-poll survey reports are often fake and planted to boost the prospects of some political parties and candidates. The code for the media in most democracies insists such reports be prefaced by conspicuously indicating the organisation which has carried out the survey, the agency which has commissioned it, the size and nature of the sample selected, the method of selection of the sample and the possible margin of error in the findings.

This minimum data has to be incorporated in the report so published to authenticate the genuineness of the survey. This is exactly what the Press Council of India (PCI) has laid down with regard to the publication of the pre-poll surveys. It is wrong to say that the PCI has asked for a blanket ban on the publication of pre-election surveys.

As regards the exit-poll surveys — conducted outside polling booths by speaking to voters coming out — the PCI has undoubtedly requested the press not to publish such surveys till

* P.B. Sawant (Chairman, Press Council of India)

the final vote has been cast in the coming election. Or, indeed, in any election. This is relevant given staggered polling.

After all, when polls are staggered, some voters, whether in an entire region of the country or merely in some constituencies or even in the same constituency — if, for example, voting in certain booths is countermanded — are still to cast their ballots. In such circumstances, when the exit poll surveys indicate that a majority of the voters has favoured some party or candidate, there is a "bandwagon" impact. The rest of the voters go with the majority. This could be simply because they feel they should be with the majority or because they realise the futility of voting for a party which has earned a minority of votes.

Such an occurrence amounts to direct interference with the choice of voters. It is not correct to equate the publication of such reports with editorial comments or reports in newspapers which may indicate that the voting has gone one way or the other. Readers are intelligent enough to know that such comments or reports are the opinion of the editor or the reporter in question and they may not have anything to do with the actual pattern of voting.

But this is not the case with the exit-poll survey reports. They tell the voters of the actual state of affairs. This is apart from the fact that there are cases of fake exit-poll reports, which are planted to influence voters.

All those interested in maintaining the purity of the electoral process will agree that this is the minimum precaution which has to be taken by those who publish poll survey reports. The duty of ensuring clean polls lies with every individual and institution — not just with the government, political parties, the Election Commission and the PCI.

The PCI had framed the guidelines as part of the Code of Journalistic Ethics as early as 1996, in pursuance of section 13(2)(b), (c) and (d) of the Press Council Act. It is fallacious to say the PCI has no legal jurisdiction in the matter. The PCI's Code of Ethics goes beyond law and restrictions placed on the freedom of speech and expression under Article 19(2) of the Constitution.

For example, when the code lays down that there should be pre-verification of facts, that there should be no mixing of comment with fact, or suppression or distortion of facts, or that newspapers and magazines must give the aggrieved party an opportunity to reply and so on, it goes beyond the requirements of law. Ethics should not be confused with law. The PCI has framed the Code of Ethics under the provisions of its parent Act. It will be justified in monitoring any violations.

8

INDEPENDENT CANDIDATES

The candidates at the election as Members of Parliament or Members of Legislative Assembly generally belong to recognised, and unrecognised parties. But besides them, a large number of candidates contest as independent candidates. Most of the candidates contesting as independent candidates, by and large are non-serious candidates, and often pose a very big problem for the Election Commission. Majority of the independent candidates forfeit their deposits, and at the same time a few could get more than 50% votes also. The relevant figures upto the year 1984 are furnished below:

Year	Candidates	Elected	Elected by 50%	Lost Deposit
1952	533	38	14	356
1957	431	42	19	289
1962	480	20	8	379
1967	864	35	8	745
1971	1,134	14	8	1,066
1977	1,224	9	6	1,190
1980	2,826	9	4	2,694
1984	3,792	5	4	3,746

The above figures clearly indicate that in the year 1984, out of 3,792 independent candidates, only 5 candidates were elected, and 3,746 lost their deposits. As against this, out of 1,521 candidates put up by the recognised political parties, 510, that is 1 in 3, were elected, and only 517 lost their deposits, giving practically the same ratio of 1 in 3.

Taking into consideration the administrative difficulties faced by the Election Commission, the Commission had been from time to time writing to the government for the elimination of the non-serious, particularly the independent candidates. This is certainly a very serious problem and deserves to be remedied without any further loss of time. The gravity of the administrative difficulty faced by the Commission, can be realised from the fact that in one of the elections, there were in one constituency as many as 308 independent candidates. Such a large number of independent candidates from one constituency do create lot of problems for the Election Commission; additional symbols have to be provided at the last minute; very long ballot papers have to be printed, many more ballot boxes are to be placed at the polling booths, and more security arrangements are to be made for the peaceful conduct of the elections. Election Commission has now made certain recommendations and has issued certain guidelines to restrict the number of non-serious independent candidates, with the hope of getting some desirable results. There is indeed a dire need to check this institution of independent candidates, and the formation of the Voters Council in each constituency can also help in bringing awareness among the voters to ignore the non-serious independent candidates, and discourage them by whatever means they can. The independent candidates have by and large done more harm than any good in the holding of fair and peaceful elections.

Barring a few most deserving and serious candidates, there is a deep rooted conspiracy in putting up large number of independent candidates. The indepth study shows that there are variety of reasons behind the fielding of large number of independent candidates. Some of these candidates are fielded by a particular candidate from a recognised or non-recognised party, for later on withdrawing from the contest in his favour, to create an atmosphere in his favour. This is sheer exploitation and an utter abuse of the process of the Election Laws. Some are fielded with a view to get a large number of counting agents, polling agents who can have entry inside the polling booths and counting booths. On the day of counting, every independent candidate with his counting agents has a free access inside the place where counting is undertaken, and they can create any sort of trouble in favour of or against any candidate for a *quid pro quo*. In some cases, it has been seen that 'booth capturing, or removal of ballot boxes, or even *maar peet* has been done through these persons, who have no stakes whatsoever.

Such type of non-serious candidates are fully compensated, and are a hinderance in holding fair and free elections. In fact criminalisation of politics starts from these very persons, who develop close relationship with a candidate for whom they work in the elections. Therefore, the institution of independent candidates has got to be discouraged at all costs and with a firm hand.

I remember a case, where I was myself present at the centre where counting was to take place. While the counting was going on, immediately at one table there was lot of noise and suddenly scuffle took place between the counting agents of both the parties. One of the counting agents, in a huff tore out some ballot papers, as his candidate was losing by a small margin. The situation aggravated to such an extent that the police had to be called, and many heads had been broken by the battons of the police. We had luckily a narrow escape, but many persons present in the hall were seriously injured. The result was, the counting had to the stopped and repoll had to be ordered which suited the candidate who had wanted some trouble to be created for a repoll. In that centre there were certainly many counting agents belonging to some independent candidates, but were working for a candidate from a recognised party.

If this type of serious mishap can take place right under the nose of the central government in the capital of India, one can imagine as to what is not possible in a remote corner of a village where there is no immediate police *bandobast* available.

9

COALITION GOVERNMENT AND THE ERA OF OUTSIDE SUPPORT

Appointment of the Prime Minister

That the President of India under the Constitution has unfettered power in the appointment of a Prime Minister. But certainly there are some well-settled guidelines and conventions, which are generally kept in mind by the President, while choosing the Prime Minister. The President, therefore, has to appoint the Prime Minister, keeping in view the intentions of the framers of the Constitution for the purpose of collective responsibility in the Lok Sabha, and for the stability of the country in a democratic manner.

The Prime Minister must essentially be an elected member of the Lok Sabha as also the Leader of the House of the People and must enjoy the transparent support, (not a support from outside) of the majority of the members of Parliament belonging to the house of people, wedded to the declared policies and programmes of the Government headed by him. The President of India in choosing a Prime Minister is further guided by the oath, which is absolutely different from other Constitutional functionarises. While making such an appointment, the President is duty bound to keep in mind the well-being of the people as also the unity, security and integrity of India.

The appointment of the Prime Minister has therefore to be traced into the practice and tradition based on British model and as per law laid down by the Supreme Court in various rulings including those reported in AIR 1974 S.C. 2192, and AIR 1971 SC 1002 and in the provisions of the Constitution of India.

This is abundantly clear from these rulings that the Prime Minister must essentially be an elected member of the House of the People. In making such an appointment, the President, therefore, has to keep in mind the principles sustained by democracy, his subjective satisfaction should be that the holder of this high and coveted office has the clear and transparent majority of the group or groups in the House of which he is the leader, and is first among equals. In other words no person who leads a minority group or a splinter group, with an assurance of fractured, temporary, malafide, quid pro quo, notional and an artificial support (i.e. support from outside) should have any moral, ethical, legal or constitutional right to govern the majority.

The Speaker of the Lok Sabha while delivering the Annual Lecture at the Oxford and Cambridge Society of India, Shri P.A. Sangama has also said "It is my personal and considered view that the Prime Minister must belong to the House of the People (Lok Sabha) that is what Parliamentary Democracy is all about". Mr. Sangama further said that when coalitions had a slender majority "the case becomes one of the tail wagging the dog" while he himself was the head of an eight-party coalition government every single moment was a moment of blackmailing. (Times of India, 22.8.1997)

For the major part of the post independence years, this country had the Prime Ministers who were duly elected by the people, and were also the leaders of the House of the People. That the present Prime Minister, Shri I.K. Gujral was a member of Rajya Sabha from Bihar (where he never lived and was never a resident of Bihar) and had entered the Parliament from back door against all constitutional norms, conventions and established practices. It is nothing but a fraud on the Constitution that a member of Rajya Sabha may advise the President who in turn is bound for the dissolution of the House, where he (Prime Minister) does not have any control whatsoever, and has no right of vote. Besides, the Prime Minister of the country is always expected to keep himself above board, and is indeed expected to honour the Constitutional mandate and duties as enshrined in Art. 51(a) of the Constitution of India being the most important citizen and the head of the executive. The framers of the Constitution never visualised that the office of the Prime Ministership shall be held by such a person who has no identity in the House of People and is ruling the country by the mischief of proxy. This is the Constitutional impropriety of the highest order. In the present case, Shri Ram Vilas Paswan was the Leader of the House and Shri I.K. Gujral was the Prime Minister. A Member of Rajya Sabha, being the Prime Minister is the Chief Executive in the Lok Sabha having no right to vote in a House of which he is the head and is supposed to have the confidence and support of the majority of the members of the House. What a mockery of the Parliamentary Democracy. The President of India had committed a serious mistake by appointing a non-entity as the Prime Minister of India. This is indeed a very unfortunate situation where such a high functionary, fails to perform his duty as prescribed by the Constitution of India, and gives the country, the office of the Prime Minister to any one not duly elected by them democratically through ballot.

In a Parliamentary Democracy, the Prime Minister emerges from Parliament. The learned authors, Wade and Bradly, in their classical work thus mention:

"There are in the United Kingdom conventional rules which limit the range of choice of a new Prime Minister. The support of the party or coalition which may be expected to command a majority in the House of Commons is a condition precedent to the acceptance of the office. And the leader of the party or coalition must essentially be a member of Parliament. That being the tradition, the appointment of a non-member as Prime Minister is out of question. As there is no law in the United Kingdom providing for the membership of House of Commons as a condition precedent to the appointment, there is perhaps on the same convention no provision in the Indian constitution. Indeed a Parliament consists of its members and the Council of Ministers is its executive. The executive cannot be headed by a non-member and consists of members. Parliament vests the supreme executive authority in its own members only."

In the entire Constitution the words Prime Minister occur only in Articles 74, 75 and 78. They merely provide (i) for his appointment by the President (ii) for the appointment of other ministers by the President on his advice (iii) that the Council of Ministers shall be collectively responsible to the House of the People (iv) that the Prime Minister shall communicate to the President all decisions of the Council of Ministers relating to the administration of the affairs of the Union and proposals for legislation (v) that he shall furnish such information relating to the administration of the affairs of the Union and proposals for legislation as the President may call for, (vi) and that if the

President so requires, he shall submit for the consideration of the Council of Ministers any matter on which a decision has been taken by a Minister but which has not been considered by the council.

Fall of Janata Government and the Role of the President

After the fall of Janata Government, the way Ch. Charan Singh was chosen as the Prime Minister exhibits a shameful drama played before the people of this country (nay the whole world) is an unfortunate act on the part of the then President who was equally under an oath under Art. 60 of the Constitution.

The President's subjective satisfaction under Art. 75(3) is very much questionable and attracted Art. 61 of the Constitution. For as long as Charan Singh was the care-taker Prime Minister the country was without any government.

H.M. Seervai, an eminent constitutional expert has dealt with this most unfortunate and shameful act in his book, "Constitutional Law of India". Vol. II, 1984 (Epilogue pp. 2706–2728).

Here are some excerpts:

In para 13 at page 2710 Seervai writes, "It should be mentioned that though Mr. Charan Singh was loud in his denunciation of Mrs. Gandhi and accused his colleagues in the Ministry of being "a bunch of impotant men" for not prosecuting her with vigour, he sought the support of her party and also the support of Congress(S) which had separated from her party because it could not agree with her authoritarian way. The support sought was that of two hostile parties and as regards the Congress(I), of a party which had made it known day in and day out, that it stood for abolishing the special courts set up by the Janata Government and for withdrawing the prosecution against Mrs. Gandhi, her son and others. It is inconceivable that Ch. Charan Singh could have really believed that the support of Mrs. Gandhi was unconditional . . . It is a matter of history and it is a matter of personal knowledge for the President that he knew precisely what Mrs. Gandhi's support was worth. In 1969 she had proposed him as a Congress candidate for election to the office of the President of India and her proposition was passed unanimously. However she proceeded to work for and secured the success of an independent candidate, Mr. V.V. Giri who was consequently elected as the President of India . . . If in the first instance it was Charan Singh's duty, before he spoke of unconditional support, to put it plainly to Mrs. Gandhi and her party that before giving their support it should be clearly understood that the special courts would not be abolished and the prosecutions would not be withdrawn. If in pursuit of his life's ambition he failed to discharge that duty, it was clearly incumbent upon the President to put that question directly to Mrs. Gandhi and to Mr. Stephen when they met him. The statement put out after the Ministry was sworn in, namely that the unconditional obligation to support Ch. Charan Singh ended once he was sworn in, had they been mentioned to or elicited by, the President would have made it clear that Ch. Charan Singh did not have the unconditional support of the Congress (I) and could not form a stable government.

(Shri I.K. Gujral too did not have unconditional support of the Congress and the CPI(M) and could not give a stable government.)

Departing from chronology, it may be mentioned that the predictable thing happened and on the morning of 20th August 1979, which had been fixed for vote of confidence in Ch. Charan Singh's Government, the Congress (I) decided to oppose the motion. Ch. Charan Singh resigned and stated that there were more important things in life than being a Prime Minister and he could not be a party to a bargain by which the special courts would be abolished and the prosecutions withdrawn. Had he put India first and his life's ambition second, he should have adopted this high moral tone before obtaining the support of Mrs. Gandhi's party. Coming as it did after he was driven from office by Mrs. Gandhi's party, his talk of moral principles was unreal.

The former Minister of External Affairs expressed the general feeling of people when he said "Politicians have become a laughing stock. They have become worse than prostitutes. How can we show our face to the world?" It may be that the whole story is not yet told. But enough is known to discuss profitably the two questions posed earlier. What are the powers of the President (a) in choosing a Prime Minister and (b) in dissolving the House of People?

The events leading upto, and following the fall of Janata Government have led people to wonder whether conventions evolved in the United Kingdom, can apply to the very different conditions, prevailing in India. The grave danger to our democratic constitution posed by defections and the means of averting that the dangers are considered later. However, since, the question whether the British conventions apply to the exercise of the President's powers must be answered in the frame work of our constitution, it is beyond doubt that those conventions clearly apply.

The President's action was clearly contrary to Art. 75(1) read with Art. 75(3) and the convention which is necessarily implied in that Article. The President ought not to have called upon a person to form a Government unless he commanded the confidence of the majority of the House of the People. If the President considered that more time was required to secure that end, more time should have been given to both the contestants before appointing any person as Prime Minister. Admittedly Ch. Charan Singh did not command a majority in the House of the People; consequently his having a large number of supporters than Mr. Desai was irrelevant. To have given him three weeks' time to find out whether he could secure the necessary majority was contrary to the principle underlying Art. 75(1) and 75(3) of the Constitution of India. The extreme importance of adhering to the principle underlying Art. 75(1) and (3) will be obvious, if the grave consequences of its breach are considered.

In any event, if the object of the President and of all the parties up to that time was to avoid a mid-term poll, it was wrong for the President not to have called upon Mr. Jagjivan Ram to form an alternative Government. The fact that the other parties to serve their own interest expressed themselves in favour of a mid term poll, when nothing had changed except that the leader of the largest party expressed his readiness and ability to form a stable government could not absolve the President from his duty to put the interests of the country above the interests of a large number of fragmented and hostile parties. It has been suggested that for the President to have called upon Mr. Jagjivan Ram as the leader of the party of 205 Janata M.Ps would have been to encourage defection. This suggestion can only be described as grotesquo after President Reddy had called upon the great defector, Ch. Charan Singh, to form a Government. As stated earlier, it is much easier for a party of 205 members to secure the necessary support in a House of 544 members than for a leader of about 75 members. It is submitted that the President's action was not only improper and discriminatory but led to a situation in which he should never have placed the country. He set up a Government which never commanded the confidence of the House of People at all, that Government was to remain in power for a period of 4 months. **The President of India has thus presented to the world the humiliating spectacle of a great democratic country being ruled by a Government which never commanded the confidence of the House of the People.**

(In the case of Sri I.K. Gujral, the situation was still worse. Neither he was a member of Lok Sabha, nor he commanded the support and confidence of majority of the House.)

Factual Position of Earlier Governments

After the independence of the country, Jawaharlal Nehru was appointed as the first Prime Minister. He ruled the country for the largest number of years, i.e. until the year 1964, when he died on 27th May. 1964. He was the unanimous choice and had the transparent support of the Congress, the single largest party.

After his unfortunate death on 27 May, 1964, Gulzari Lal Nanda was appointed as the acting Prime Minister. He continued as such till Lal Bahadur Shastri was chosen as the CPP Leader. After having been chosen as the Leader of the House the President appointed him as the next Prime Minister having confidence and unconditional support from the majority party in the House.

After the unfortunate death of Lal Bahadur Shastri, Smt. Indira Gandhi was elected as the leader of the CPP. She was thus appointed as the next Prime Minister. She also continued for a very long period, with a break after emergency when the Congress party lost majority in the Lok Sabha election in the year 1977.

In 1977, when Janata Party won the election, Morarji Desai was elected as the leader of the party, and was thus appointed the Prime Minister by the President as per the provisions of the Constitution.

Era of Outside Support

In the year 1979, as has been discussed above, constitutional crises came to the surface in a very big way, when President Sanjiva Reddy appointed Ch. Charan Singh as the next Prime Minister without properly testifying the support, which he claimed to have with him. It was a malafide support from outside assured by Mrs. Indira Gandhi, who wanted to politically finish Charan Singh and forever. The President of India, according to H.M. Seervai, used his hostile discretion, knowing fully well that the hostile parties could not give unconditional support from outside. The era of outside support thus started from Charan Singh's Government.

After the death of Smt. Indira Gandhi, in the year 1984, Rajiv Gandhi was appointed as the next Prime Minister, by President Zail Singh. Unfortunately the President ignored all the provisions of the Constitution and administered him oath of the office of the Prime Minister without his being declared as the leader of the Congress Parliamentary Party.

After Rajiv Gandhi, V.P. Singh became the Prime Minister with outside support by Bhartiya Janata Party.

After the fall of V.P. Singh's Government when BJP withdrew its support, Chandra Shekhar was appointed as the Prime Minister with the outside support of Congress party. But this support could not last longer, and Chandra Shekhar had to tender his resignation on the withdrawal of support by the Congress party headed by Rajiv Gandhi. President R. Venkataraman in his book "My Presidential Years" admits his mistake.

To quote: "I did not accept the resignation without feeling sorry for Chandra Shekhar. The office hungry coterie of the Congress Party used to misguide Rajiv Gandhi that Chandra Shekhar's attempts at building up a good image could prove deleterious of his image. Looking back after two years, I realize my naiveness in accepting Congress assurance of unconditional support to last a year at least. I realised that unequal combinations are always disadvantageous to the weaker side.

I was fed up with all these experiments of running minority governments and sick of promises from outside support to them (pp. 482–484)".

The appointment of Deve Gowda as the Prime Minister, was nothing but a mockery of Democracy. And the President failed to use his descretion as per provisions of the Constitution in the right direction. While withdrawing the outside support, the President of the Congress party, Shri Sita Ram Kesari called Deve Gowda, Nikamma (inefficient) and condemned him on the floor of the House in so many words. Parliament debates on the "no-confidence motion" against Shri Deve Gowda Govt. are very revealing and put a flood of light on the whole unfortunate episode of Indian political history.

And the appointment of Shri I.K. Gujral, as Prime Minister immediately after the fall of Deve Gowda Govt. in which he himself was the External Affairs Minister, is nothing but a fraud on the Constitution. He had been appointed Prime Minister with the outside support from the same party (Congress Party) which was the main actor in pulling down the Govt. of Deve Gowda of which he himself was a senior Minister.

Soon after the appointment of Shri I.K. Gujral as Prime Minister, the Congress Party and the CPI(M) had started threatening the Gujral Govt. to withdraw their support. The national newspapers had been full of criticism of the Gujral Govt. by the supporting parties i.e. Congress and the CPI(M). The recent threat issued by the Congress President Mr. Sita Ram Kesari was reported in many national newspapers "Mr. Sita Ram Kesari today predicted the fall of the United Front Govt."

"I do not believe that this 13 party government will last" he told a Congress workers conference here (Patna)".

(*Statesman* 10/9/1997)

Don't take Congress for granted Kesari tells United Front

"Congress President Sita Ram Kesari today expressed doubts about the longevity of the United Front Government and said coalition governments were not in the interest of country. The United Front's 13 party government had inherent contradictions which made the task of its survival daunting . . ."

He strongly defended his decision to withdraw support from H.D. Deve Gowda Ministry".

(*Economic Times* 10/9/1997)

In rebuttal the Prime Minister Shri I.K. Gujral had said, "the coalition politics in the country has come to stay, and that it had helped considerably in reducing tensions between the Centre and the states . . ."

Mr. Gujral's remarks made during his address at the two day Janata Dal National Executive, assume significance, as in the context of Congress President Sita Ram Kesari's observations that a coalition government at the Centre did not serve the country's interest".

(*The Times of India* 11/9/1997)

That the grounds of withdrawal of support by the Congress party, headed by Shri Sita Ram Kesari were fully prepared, and a letter of withdrawal of support by Congress Party ultimately reached the Rashtrapati Bhawan. Thus that was the end of the Gujral Government, and the country was pushed into mid-term poll, without completing the full term of the 11th Lok Sabha.

That the outside support by any political party is unknown to the Constitution. The past experience of outside support to the governments has also shown miserable results. A writ petition was filed by this writer (Dr. Janak Raj Jai vs. Prime Minister of India and another—CWP No. 1861/97) in the High Court of Delhi, challenging the validity of the outside support to the Gujral Government.

Unfortunately the court could not decide this matter on merit, before the Congress Party withdrew its support and the Gujral Government had ultimately fallen, as it had virtually been reduced to a minority in the House. Now the whole case is in the people's court since the elections for the 12th Lok Sabha are quite at hand. The Indian voters, who are certainly at the horns of a dilemma, have to seriously think whether they want a stable government with a decisive mandate, or an instable government by giving a fractured mandate thereby putting the country in further gloom and darkness.

***Parting note:* Had the congress under the leadership of Sita Ram Kesari, joined the Gujral Government by sharing collective responsibility as per constitutional provisions, the government would not have fallen, and the country would have been saved from the present mid-term elections. It is unfortunate that Mr. Kesari chose to pull down the Gujral Government on a Sham alibi.**

PM under Strain in a Coalition: Sangma

New Delhi: Lok Sabha Speaker P.A. Sangma said here on Friday that the status of the Prime Minister was under considerable strain in a coalition government because of pressure from comparatively smaller coalition partners.

"In a coalition government, particularly in our context, the status of the Prime Minister comes under considerable strain.

Prime Ministers and Chief ministers are driven to function less autonomously than under single-party rule because of pressures even from comparatively smaller coalition constituents," Mr. Sangma said.

Delivering the annual lecture at the Oxford and Cambridge Society of India on "The Speaker and governance through coalitions," Mr. Sangma said when coalitions had a rather slender majority, "the case becomes one of the tail wagging the dog."

"This has serious implications for decision-making in government, which, in turn, manifests itself in the business of Parliament," Mr. Sangma said, adding that on the issue of floor management, he had to repeatedly remind the United Front government that he was not the parliamentary affairs minister.

Further, coalition partners co-operating at the Central level may find themselves at loggerheads at the state level in regard to certain economic issues, Mr. Sangma said, citing the example of the "clash of interests" between the DMK and Janata Dal on the sharing of the Cauvery waters despite being partners of the United Front.

Recounting his experience as the head of an eight-party coalition government in the north-eastern state, Mr. Sangma said, "every single moment was a moment of blackmailing."

He said the interest of a party in a coalition at the Centre could be inconsistent with its interest in the state, leading to conflict of interests between national-level leadership of the party and the state-level party functionaries.

Mr. Sangma said the Prime Minster must belong to Lok Sabha and not the Upper House as is in the case of Mr. I.K. Gujral or his predecessor H.D. Deve Gowda.

"It is my personal opinion and considered view that the Prime Minster must belong to the House of the People (Lok Sabha), that is what parliamentary democracy is all about," Mr. Sangma said in response to a question about the "disturbing" trend of Prime Ministers preferring the Rajya Sabha.

(*The Times of India*, 23.8.1997)

REFERENCE

1. *Constitutional Law of India* by H.M. Seervai, published by N.M. Tripathi Pvt. Ltd., Bombay.

10

INDUSTRY FOR STABLE GOVERNMENT AFTER THE POLLS

Mr. L.M. Thapar, CMD, BILT

What we need today is political stability, end of uncertainty and restoration of business.

I sincerely hope that a stable Government will emerge, either a single party Government or a coalition Government led by major party without outside support. Such a Government will bring about much needed psychological change and help in greater flow of investment both domestic and foreign.

The new Government will have to address pressing issues the economy is facing at present, namely industrial slow down, continued slump in the capital market and low rate of export growth. It has to take short term measures to put the economy back on the rails.

While it is difficult to predict the shape of the economy in 1988, I have no doubt that if stable Government emerges and appropriâte and effective measures are taken on the economic front, recovery should be visible in the latter half of 1998.

Mr. Shekhar Bajaj CMD, Bajaj Electricals

I expect a coâlition Government.

Firstly the Government must increase capital purchase which will in turn increase demand for cement, steel and other items and expedite clearances of infrastructure projects. Secondly there is need to improve the general atmosphere. To boost up exports and to support local industries, the benefit available on advance licence should be increased and the Rupee can be allowed to further devalue to around Rs. 42 to a dollar by March 1998. To accelerate economic reforms, there should be reduction in subsidies, reservation for small-scale industries should be slowly removed and all sectors must compete freely with each other.

Mr. Vikram Thapar, Joint MD, BILT

Had I been asked this question a fortnight ago, I would have said "A Coalition Government". Last week, asked this same question, I would have replied. "A Single Party", and, today, I would reply with the words "Coalition" once again. I think the situation is too fluid at this point of time to give a reasoned assessment but, in all likelihood, I would expect that we will see a coalition Government of all like-minded parties possibly linked through a pre-election alliance.

Mr. Manmohan Singh as Finance Minister, had assured that we would maintain a rupee-dollar parity rate after accounting for the disparity between domestic and international inflation. In other words, if the domestic rate of inflation was 5 per cent higher than the international inflation "standard" the rupee would devalue by a like amount so that our exports would continue to be competitive, and the tariff structure continue at a uniform rate. But I would suggest inclusion of account for the actual cost of money in determining the exchange rate. If the net effective cost of borrowing in India today is approximately 10 per cent, while the international norm is 3 per cent, then, to level the playing field, the exchange rate of the rupee should be valued taking into account both factors, the actual inflationary differential alongwith the monetary differential between the Indian economy and the "standard" of the global economy. This would immediately reactive exports and kick start industrial activity.

I doubt if the new Government would be able to implement the steps needed to revitalise the economy before the beginning of the 3rd quarter of 1998, and since results of their actions will only follow several months later, 1998 is not going to be a picnic. Having written off 1996 and praised the Lord for ending 1997, I regret that I do not look forward to 1998 with a great optimism.

Mr. K.P. Singh, Chairman, MD DLF Universal Limited

Though my preference would have been for a one party Government, it may not be feasible in the present context. I expect a coalition Government of like-minded parties and definitely not one with outside support to emerge after the elections.

I would expect the Government to take following measures to revive the economy:

Restore public confidence; Expedite completion to reform process; Increase public investment in infrastructure sector; Downsize Government expenditure; Bring in greater transparency in Government functioning; Stimulate demand through a thrust in those sectors of economy which can quickly lead to its take off such as Housing and Construction Sector that has been recognised as the engine to kick start the economy.

I would suggest increase in public expenditure on development activities particularly infrastructure sector even if that means marginal increase in fiscal deficit. Besides we must adhere to WTO no more or less.

I do not expect Indian economy to turn the corner in 1998. However, if the new Government gets down to business right away and gives full attention to develop the economy, I expect an economic recovery towards the end of 1998.

Mr. Kulwant Rai, Chairman Emeritus, Usha Group

Coalition Government at the Centre depending on outside support has failed. People are fed up with continued political instability. This has done immense harm to the country. I sincerely hope that in the forthcoming Lok Sabha elections, people will give a clear verdict in favour of a single party. This is necessary to bring about political and economic stability.

The revival of industrial activity and stepping up of exports should be the top agenda of the new government. I have no doubt that single party government supported by like-minded smaller groups will bring about the much needed policy changes. The new government will be in a position to take hard economic decisions such as speeding up economic reforms, passage of pending economic bills, increase in capital expenditure particularly in infrastructure sector, measures to stimulate demand and pruning of non-development expenditure.

Dr. N.M. Dhuldhoya Vice-CMD, NOCIL

Coalition governments are a reflection of changing times. They herald a new era for Indian democracy. Indian democracy in its growing maturity has nurtured an electorate that has become extremely sensitive, discerning and selective. The fact that coalition governments in India have been able to deliver, sometimes better and quicker than single party governments, has made the electorate comfortable with the concept.

The new government should reverse the industrial slow down by reviving the confidence of industrial segments that were badly beaten by the swift pace of liberalisation and the ensuing competition. Accordingly there is need for a comprehensive, unbiased, anomaly-free policy for domestic industry to ensure genuine level playing field in areas of taxation, commercial borrowing and administered prices. The pace of industrial reforms must synchronise with the pace of globalisation and tariff reforms. The capital market needs to be revived more specifically the primary market, which has been dormant after the collapse in 1995. In the wake of the steep currency devaluation ranging from 35 to 75 per cent in the SE Asian countries, there is no alternative but to improve the productivity and value-addition of our exports with focus on brand-building for long-term survival.

Mr. Ajay S. Shriram, Vice-CMD, DCM Shriram Consolidated

I expect a coalition Government, as now a large number of regional/smaller political parties have been formed. These parties draw their members from the few large political parties, consequently reducing the base of the larger parties. I do hope all the coalition partners would be in the Government as any party giving outside support can influence the decision making process without taking responsibility for the consequences.

A pre-requisite for any industrial activity and economic growth is a stable Government. The sooner this is established, better will be the process of revival of Indian industry.

It is doubtful if the economy will turn the corner in 1998. There are too many uncertainties at this stage. The stability and confidence has to be rebuilt and a year may be too short for a complete turn around.

Mr. L. Lakshman Assochem President

We need a stable Government, either single party Government or a coalition led by major party. The coalition Government should not be based on outside support. In my view political parties should arrive at broad national consensus on economic policies so that economic development does not suffer on account of political instability.

The new Government should set a target of 8 per cent GDP growth over the next five years; industrial, agricultural and service sector growth of 11 per cent, 4 per cent and 10 per cent respectively; gross domestic savings ratio to 30 per cent of GDP; reduction of fiscal deficit to 2.5 per cent and aggregate subsidies to 5 per cent of GDP by 2003, resource mobilisation of Rs. 100,000 crores over the next five years through privatisation of PSUs, 100 per cent adult literacy and containing population growth to 1 per cent by 2010.

I would suggest deregulation and selective corporatisation of agriculture, large investment in rural infrastructure and improving credit delivery mechanism and improving credit delivery mechanism and marketing infrastructure. In the industrial sector, all non-strategic industries should be delicensed, steps should be taken to revitalise Indian industry, evolve code against hostile takeovers by foreign companies, strengthen antidumping and safeguard mechanism and facilitate foreign direct investment to supplement domestic resources.

To have world class infrastructure, it is necessary to corporatise transmission and distribution of electricity to bring about financial viability of SEBs, evolve uniform and transparent regulatory framework for independent power producers, further deregulate telecom and energy sector, open the mining sector, particularly coal, allow participation of private sector in development of ports and modernisation of shipping facilities. The Government should formulate policy of civil aviation, to announce fresh initiatives for urban infrastructure development and building of express ways connecting the four Metros.

Mr. H.S. Singhania CMD, JK Corp.

I look to 1998 with hope that it will give us a strong and stable Government, alive to the realities of the Indian economic scene, and which will do everything possible to help Indian industry at this difficult period and temper economic globalisation to suit our own needs. Urgent effective measures are necessary to boost demand and instill confidence in the Indian corporate sector. The international economic scenario is likely to become even more difficult as a fall out of the happenings in South East Asia and the turmoil in the Japanese economy. This would require apt, flexible, realistic and quick responses as well as proactive actions. I wish we would have at the helm of affairs a team of economic policy makers equal to the task. There is no dearth of entrepreneurs or entrepreneurship in India or people ready to take risks. Indian business have no small dreams, but for their big dreams to fructify, India Incorporated must evolve and work.

wrong in equipping the voter with information so that he can decide what is best for him?

Next, some "ban men" say, "The sample is too small." Yet others say, in dark asides, "These guys are all available for a price"—and they should know! In fact, most national opinion polls have samples of well over 10,000. Are the "ban men" aware that when an opinion pollster gets the results wrong, his normal commercial business is adversely affected?

Would a reputable organisation risk 98 per cent of its business—for most market research companies, election surveys comprise no more than 2 to 3 per cent of their business—to take a chance on an inadequate sample? No way. Also, would a publication like, say, *India Today* risk an inadequate sample or a disreputable agency? No way, I would say, even without checking with the editor.

"But they do get it wrong, don't they?" say the "ban men" gleefully. Of course they do—sometimes; and not only in India but the world over. All samples have an error. Do the "ban men" know that a 1 per cent swing in votes for a major all-India party means a difference of 15–20 seats in the Lok Sabha?

So a good forecast with an error of plus or minus 3 per cent could mean that a party gets 45–60 more seats—or fewer. So the party wins or loses an election on that 3 per cent. It's a tough business, friends—both yours and ours.

What would be the result of banning polls after campaigning for, say, a general election begins? First, you would be left with old results that do not take into account the effects of the campaigning. Second, there would be clandestine leaks by politicians of conflicting results of polls that may not even have been conducted. No reputable polling agency would be named and no major publication would put its name on the line. So the public would be at the mercy of quacks, charlatans and crooks with nothing to lose.

Thus, there is little to commend this utterly ill-conceived and retrograde step of banning election forecasts, even if it were legal to do so. Incidentally, under which part of Article 19(2) of the Constitution would the ban be sought? Would it be for reasons of "security of state" or "public order" or would it be for "decency or morality"?

As far as exit polls are concerned, there is absolutely no case for banning them. Admittedly, there may be a case for withholding the results—as pollsters have often voluntarily done—until the completion of voting.

tionship as an important factor in the generation of black money. V.V. Giri, the Hon'ble President of India himself said in his message to the Nation on the eve of Independence Day 1974:

> "It has been a most regrettable development in recent years that money power has come to play such a dominant role in the election to legislatures. This, to my mind, is the root of corruption and corrupt influences in our public life. People may lose faith in cherished democratic values if leaders of all political parties do not take prompt correct measures to remedy the situation by Government consultation."

Some years later, M.C. Chagla, a former Chief Justice of Bombay High Court, a Union Minister and a Jurist said,:

> "The elected members do not represent the people, they represent money power."

It has been rightly observed that "Looking at the picture as a whole, it has to be recognised that the weakness of the political parties is a major infirmity in the working of our political system today; with a few exceptions, the organisation of fragile parties is fragile and they are unable to command curable loyalities.

Multiplicity of Parties

No other democratic country has such a multiplicity of parties, with the possibility of their number increasing any time through the spliting of the existing parties or formation of new ones without any distinctive policy or viable programme. Nor is it easy to find instances in other well functioning democracies of such uncontrolled flow of funds to parties from undisclosed sources.

The Election Commission of India, in its report on the general election to the Legislative Assemblies in 1979, and House of People in 1980, listed what it considered disturbing trends in the internal affairs of the parties and had observed that in the interest of proper functioning of the parties, which is vitally necessary for the survival of democratic institutions, a law should be made by Parliament providing for among other things, compulsory registration of political parties, regulating their internal

In one of the judgements, in which political parties moved the High Court for approval of the amendment of their Memorandum of Association to include an object of making contribution to political parties, Justice M.C. Chagla said, " Democracy should be looked after, tended and nurtured, so that it should rise to its full and proper stature."

A party — usually the party in power which commands large financial resources, is not disposed of to consider the problem of funding of election campaign, to be one of great importance or urgency. The parties which are not in a position to command such resources, would, and have in fact attached far greater importance all these years to this problem and to prevention of lavish expenditure on election campaign. Quite understandably, these parties are acutely conscious of the use and abuse of money on elections and have generally regarded state funding as the most important of the measures likely to achieve, to the extent possible, equality of opportunity in election contests.

Mr. P.J. Kurian a member of parliament raised this issue in Parliament. To quote, " in the eighties debate took place on the question of state funding of election. In fact, I had moved a private Member Bill in the Lok Sabha, around this period. Unfortunately, we did not pursue this debate and, therefore, no serious proposal to make it a reality emerged. I believe it is the high time that we give serious thought to this proposal. Of course, when the State funds the election, no candidate should be allowed to spend any money. It is a matter of common knowledge that huge amount of black money finds its way into the election expenses and vitiates the economy apart from corruption in the electoral system. This cannot go on. We have to cry a halt somewhere. We must learn to change the present noisy, high profile election campaign into a more sobre and issue based campaign."

As early as in 1964, when the growth of black money was at an incipient stage and the political parties were generally still observing ethical norms, the Santhanam. Committee on Prevention of Corruption sounded a warning. It observed that the existence of large amounts of unaccounted black money was a major source of corruption. The black economy continued to ramify and the relationship between it and politics, especially demands for funds to finance election campaigns also continued to grow. In 1971, the Wanchoo Committee identified the rela-

11

THE REAL PROBLEM AND ITS POSSIBLE REMEDIES

The Election Commission of India has issued a Notification declaring the General Elections for the 12th Lok Sabha in the country, beginning from 16th February, 1998. The representatives already elected by the people through the ballot could not complete the five year term. After the fall of the two Governments within less than two years, due to in-fighting and bad governance, they are back again before the voters, seeking a fresh mandate. As to who is to blame for this chaotic situation, entirely depends on the Indian voter to decide. The voter is the real master of the destiny of country in a democratic set up. Here is an interesting description as to who was responsible to create the situation for fresh elections."Prospect of elections drives MPs to tears." Together they would have liked to sing — *Aa ab laut chalen* (Let us go back now). But the question worth several hundred crores of rupees — the cost of holding election — is whether there can be any going back now. The political situation is indeed chaotic. But Prime Minister I.K. Gujral and leader of the Opposition Atal Behari Vajpayee on Monday turned poetic. It was the choicest of Hindustani poetry.

Emotional scenes before dissolution of 11th Lok Sabha

Should the eleventh Lok Sabha — sent into 'Coma' by the Speaker — be finally dissolved, there will be a lot many losers in the coming days. The worst affected would be the first timers in the Lok Sabha, who would not be eligible for pension. Holding a meeting at Parliament House Annexe, two scores of them

literally knocked at the gates of Rashtrapati Bhawan. Mr. Sangama's 'Shock Therapy' of adjourning the Lok Sabha sine-die has had the effect of ending all prospects for the present at least of a discussion on the Jain Panel Report . . . As the country seems to be hurtling towards a general election, serious second thoughts are being nursed by many of those directly affected. Mr. Sharad Pawar, for instance remains a votary of the 'find some way out'.

The writing on the wall is clear enough. The people may give yet another mixed verdict and the 12th Lok Sabha may require another experiment at governance by coalition. (Mr. P.P. Rao, Senior Advocate of the Supreme Court in his recent article had also predicted a hung Parliament after the 12th Lok Sabha Elections). Public posturing apart, the fact is that no MP wants an election but he blames it on his peers and the peers blame each other. There lies the tragedy.*

People's Dilemma

People belonging to different schools of thought, particularly the non politicians (Doctors, Educationists, Journalists, Engineers, Industrialists, Lawyers etc.) are in a great dilemma and are looking for a remedy which may give a stable government and good governance to the country. After the era of outside support, unholy alliances, *raajneeti* of *joar-toar* (politics of convenience), formation of coalition governments, criminalisation in politics, and frequent dissolution of the Lok Sabhas prematurely, have become the order of the day and the foundation of all the democratic institutions have been shaken beyond repair. There has been a big question mark on the creditability of the institutions like, parliament, judiciary, bureaucracy, police etc. The Indian voter today is completely baffled, and is completely reduced to be a silent spectator. Inspite of the fact that he casts his vote to the best of his knowledge and full sense of responsibility, he stands betrayed by his own representative whom he sends to the Parliament or the Assembly. To his utter dismay, his elected representative keeps on changing colours for a quid pro-quo. It is here that something very seriously has got to be done, to bring drastic improvements in the present electoral system to bring stability and good governance in the country.

* Times of India, dated 25.11.1997.

The task is gigantic and not an easy one, but yet earnest efforts by all and sundry must continue. The time and space at our disposal are not adequate to discuss this problem elaborately in this small book, which is being brought out at such a short notice so as to reach every voter before the commencement of the election. But still we have made an earnest effort to give as much material as possible for the information and guidance of the voters who are in dire need, to act in the right direction at the 12th Lok Sabha Election.

Justice G.T. Nanavati

The political situation has become so chaotic that even one of the judges of the Highest Court (Justice G.T. Nanavati) did not hesitate to express his views publically in a Seminar organised by Senior Lawyers at the India International Centre, the topic being — The Role of Judiciary in Good Governance. To quote: "Fifty years have passed since independence, but what have we achieved during this time? It can be said without hesitation that we do not have good governance even after such a long period. The state of affairs in the country has led to growing sense of frustration and despair. High expectations have given way to pessimism born out of misery, corruption, criminalisation and deterioration of moral values of life. The conduct of our elected representatives to various legislative and governing bodies and the manner in which our executives exercise their power have shaken the very faith of the people in the institute of governance." Dr. Kashyap, who was associated with the parliament for over 37 years and served as the Secretary General of the Lok Sabha for some time, has very aptly described the situation: "Those in government are so pre-occupied with the struggle for survival in power that they have no time for addressing their attention to the problems of the people. There has been sharp erosion in the respect that people have for politicians. In many parts of the country, the government simply does not exist. Mafia gangs terrorise and rule, with the thin line fast disappearing between politicians and criminals."

The concept of good governance is not new. Our ancient scriptures like Mahabharata, Ramayana, Kautilya's Arthashastra and many of our classics and those from other foreign countries have spelt out what is good governance. It is essentially

conducting the State Affairs in such a way as to result in maximum good for the masses at large.

Judiciary like the Legislature and the executive has an important role to play in good governance. One of the roles of the judiciary is to check the wrongful acts of the legislature and the executive. By keeping a check over the legislature and the executive in this manner, the judiciary performs its role in the good governance of the people of this country. The powers given to the High Courts and the Supreme Court are fairly wide and sufficient to keep the legislature and the executive under check. Judiciary can contribute to good governance by striking down the legislative and executive acts which tend to impinge upon the basic human rights and liberty of the citizens. No doubt, the judiciary has been actively involved in this role. But, new ways and means can still be found to give more bite to the judicial functioning.

For effective governance we must have quality leaders. And quality leadership can be provided by persons who are trained to look at things objectively.

Unless we have good leaders to represent the citizens of this country in the Legislature or in the executive, we cannot have good governance."

India, no doubt, is a country which has been governed by too many laws with little justice mainly on account of the delay oriented procedures. That is the main reason that our country has been able to do precious little to provide social, economic and political justice to the millions of poor and downtrodden people. The main cause for this degeneration, therefore, is the deterioration of the quality of leadership. It is thus the need of the hour that the judges, lawyers and other intellectuals of the society actively take part in the governance of the country. Then and then only the quality of the leadership will improve and the country would get good governance through able and stable Government.

Urging the political parties to give ticket to educated and civilised persons without any tainted record, in the coming elections, President of the Senior Advocates Association, Dr. V.N. Saraf said, "the criminal turned politicians syndicate and mafia organisations having links with the Government functionaries and with the political mentors have ruined the country's social, economic and democratic fabric."

Quoting Election Commission records, Dr. Saraf further said 40 M.Ps and 700 MLAs, elected to Parliament and State Assemblies last time were facing trials in the courts for involvement in as many as 4,027 criminal cases.

Plea for non Official Observers

Former Chief Justice of High Court of Delhi, and President Peoples Union of Civil Liberties has written to the Election Commission of India, asking it to consider the issue of authorising non-official observers in the forthcoming general elections.

Mr. Justice (Retd) Sachhar has also written to several political parties including the Janata Dal, BJP, CPI, CPM, Congress and the United Front seeking their views and support on this issue. Chairing the discussions organised by the Capital Foundation of India, Mr. Justice Sachhar contended that, "When in a country like Pakistan, which is going through such turmoil, unofficial poll observers could be appointed then the same could be applied in India as well."

Participating in the Discussion, Prof. Bhim Singh said, "the number of PILs filed in various courts against criminalisation of parties spoke volumes about the state of affairs in India."*

Appeal by Eminent Citizens to Bar Criminals from Polls

Eminent citizens including Vice-President Krishan Kant's wife Suman Krishan Kant have urged political parties not to give tickets to convicted persons in the coming Lok Sabha polls to rid politics of criminalisation. In a letter, duly signed by Ajit Bhattacharya, M.G. Menon, Ved Marwah, A.M. Khusro, Kapila Hingorani, Rajinder Puri, Rajinder Sachhar, A.P. Venkateshwaran, and Maya Daruwala, they have urged all the recognised national parties to:

(a) ensure strict compliance with Section 8B of the Representation of the People Act disqualifying a convicted person, including those on bail or on appeal, from contesting elections.

(b) adopt a declared and transparent process for screening out undesirable candidates and ensure nominations only to

* Statesman — 4.1.98.

those well known for their honesty, integrity and track record of proven public service.

(c) get sworn affidavits from candidates stating that they are not charged with any offence involving moral turpitude, or disclose to the public details of any cases pending against them.

(d) pointing out that a high proportion of women candidates contesting elections were successful, the network said that in the last general election one in every 13 women contestants won as against one out of 27 male candidates.

"It is incumbent on you that the orders passed by the Election Commission are obeyed implicitly. The further adoption and implementation of the transparent screening and public information process outlined above, together with an equal opportunity for representation provided to women, will make a critical difference for the achievement of clean politics and governance, the crying need of the country, the network said."

State Funding

It has also been suggested that in order to avoid the misuse of money power, for conducting free and fair election, there should be a State Funding. Raja Vishwanath Pratap Singh, has always been a strong votary of this provision. Our present Prime Minister, Sh. I.K. Gujral, also belongs to this School of thought. In one of his articles, written years back he said, "Every system has to pay for the polity that it has chosen. The Kings and Sovereigns get their privy purses and the army based dictatorships have their own funding systems. If for good reasons the country has opted in favour of multiparty system, there is no reason why it should not be a charge on the exchequer. This may not eliminate unhealthy practices altogether, but once the minimum must have been provided for, it becomes easier to enforce political ethics."

Bane of Power

The nexus between money bags and politicians is a matter of great concern not only in India, but the whole world. Money and mafia have entered the political field in such a great measure, that it has become a cancerous disease.

functioning and the manner and mode of election of their office bearers and other committees at various levels at regular intervals.

While addressing at the Institute of Constitutional and Parliamentary Studies the then Chief Election Commissioner stated that, "unless the role of political parties so far as it concerned elections, was properly regulated, any attempt directed towards the furtherance of the purity of elections would be frustrated. Accordingly he proceeded to make the following suggestions:

> The election law should confine itself to the functioning of 'Political Parties' and the broad parameters of their working, the law empowering the election commission, to work out the details of regulating measures relating to:
>
> (i) compulsory registration of political parties;
> (ii) compulsory maintenance of accounts, including all receipts and donations, minutes books etc.;
> (iii) open acceptance of donation from companies and individuals under proper receipts subject to suitably regulatory condition, including tax relief with ceiling in the case of individual donors;
> (iv) compulsory audit of account by agency to be nominated by the commission;
> (v) submission of periodical reports to the commission;
> (vi) residuary matter relating to the role of political parties;

The said paper, which the Chief Election Commissioner read out at the institute, was also circulated to all the political parties, by way of feeler to get the reaction of the parties. Reacting to the suggestions made in the paper, E.M.S. Namboodripad said, "the expenditure during an election campaign provided to a party an opportunity for educating the public mind on public issues and policies and performances, any expenditure that a party may incur on this entirely legitimate activity, ought not to be linked up with the permissible expenditure of individual candidate of the party."

Inspite of all the draw-backs in the system of holding the elections that we have witnessed during the long span of 50 years, we must admit the fact that election is the cornerstone of democracy. And the stability of the democratic system depends in the fairness of the elections held throughout the country, as and when the occassion arises. It goes without saying that de-

mocracy, under no circumstances can survive in the absence of free and fair elections. If the elections are vitiated, by violence, intimidation, booth capturing and other unfair and corrupt practices, the choice of the people is not properly reflective and the democracy thus becomes a sheer mockery, and a fraud on the constitution.

The voter is the final master and the judge of the people's court. But his choice is limited. He has to elect a candidate to represent his constituency from among those who are selected by the political parties, or who contest the election as independent candidates. It is, therefore, the sacred duty of every political party to field candidates of outstanding qualities, with dynamic manifestoes, taking into consideration the welfare of the millions of the poor and downtrodden people of the country. For a healthy democracy, and for the welfare and uplift of the poverty stricken people, we must have a healthy parliament and legislative assemblies with true and dedicated representatives duly elected by the people and for the people.

Appeal to the Voter

Before I conclude, here is an earnest appeal in the name of an Indian voter, in whose hands the destiny of the country lies.

1. Vote is a trust with you.
2. You are the judge, who must deliver judgement in favour of the right representative of your choice.
3. Vote you must. In case you fail to do so, you fail to have a government that gives a good governance.
4. Vote independently, impartially and with free and fair mind.
5. While casting your precious and valuable vote, always keep the country's interest above your own personal and individual interest.
6. Remember, you always get the government you deserve.
7. The value of the vote is the same between the prince and the pauper. Even if you are the poor of poorest, the price of your vote does not diminish.
8. The elite class, the judges, the lawyers, the educationists, the industrialists, the Doctors, the Engineers, and the bureaucrats must come out to cast the vote and fully participate in the formation of a stable government that completes the full term.

9. If you have your own conveyance do carry as many voters as you can to the polling booth.
10. Clear mandate only will give a stable government and good governance.
11. Fractured mandate weakens all the institutions, and encourages unhealthy and unholy alliances, and ultimately results in premature dissolution of Parliament.
12. Do not take it for granted that if you fail to put a cup of milk in the tank, the tank still will be full of milk. Similarly if you do not reach the ballot box and cast your precious vote, you will not get the government that you wish to have.
13. Your first preference should be a national party, and the second preference should be the merits of the candidate.
14. Do not — repeat — do not vote a candidate whose credentials are doubtful, or who has a tainted or shady character, even though he/she belongs to a national party.
15. Do not cast your vote in favour of a candidate who is contesting from more than one Constituency.
16. Do not cast a vote in favour of a candidate, who changes his earlier Constituency.

The author and the publisher will be extremely happy if the voter derives any light and benefit through this work, in solving the dilemma as to why and to whom should he/she cast his/her most valuable vote in giving a quality leadership for a quality governance. Remember, there are no soft options for a hard decision.

Over to the voters who are the real masters of the destiny of their motherland — India.

REFERENCE

1. *Journal of Constitutional and Parliamentary Studies*, January–June, 1994, p. 249.

12

"LET'S EQUIP THE VOTER"*

Prohibit polls—and allow quacks, charlatans and crooks to mislead people

Ban Opinion Polls after Campaigning begins", shrieks one headline. "Say no to exit polls", howls another. All this brouhaha is the outcome of the meetings that the Election Commission (EC) has held with various political parties. It is a matter of no surprise—but of considerable regret—that while the three wise men at Nirvachan Sadan (the EC's headquarters in Delhi) were busy meeting a cross-section of political parties and personalities, they did not deem it necessary to invite leading opinion polling organisations to present the other side of the case. So much for the scientific temper, the dedication to fairness and, if I may add, the wisdom of the EC.

What are the objections that most political parties have put forward for the banning of opinion polls once campaigning begins?

"Opinion polls influence voting behaviour, so they should be banned," say the "ban men", if I may be permitted a neologism. Some studies have suggested that there is a bandwagon effect—people rushing to support the winner. Others claim that there is an underdog effect—voters backing the apparent loser. But is there any consistent evidence to support the contention that opinion polls have a net influence on voting behaviour? No. Moreover, most of India's polls are carried in the press—mainly English-language press-whose reach is quite limited.

Yet, opinion polls do help strategic voting. For instance, if the poll shows that the candidate of my preferred party has no hope, I may move my vote to my second preference. But what's

*Dorab R. Sopariwala